FRIEDRICH NIETZSCHE

THOUGHTS
OUT OF SEASON

PART II

THE USE AND ABUSE OF HISTORY
SCHOPENHAUER AS EDUCATOR

TRANSLATED BY
ADRIAN COLLINS, M. A.

LONDON: GEORGE ALLEN & UNWIN LTD.
RUSKIN HOUSE, 40 MUSEUM STREET, W.C. 1
NEW YORK: THE MACMILLAN COMPANY

First Published 1909
Reprinted . 1910
   „   . 1913
   „   . 1927

Printed in Great Britain by
THE EDINBURGH PRESS, EDINBURGH

To L. P.

CONTENTS.

INTRODUCTION.

THE two essays translated in this volume form the second and third parts of the *Unzeitgemässe Betrachtungen*. The essay on history was completed in January, that on Schopenhauer in August, 1874. Both were written in the few months of feverish activity that Nietzsche could spare from his duties as Professor of Classical Philology in Bâle.

Nietzsche, who served in an ambulance corps in '71, had seen something of the Franco-German War, and to him it was the "honest German bravery" that had won the day. But to the rest of his countrymen it was a victory for German culture as well; though there were still a few elegancies, a few refinements of manners, that might veneer the new culture, and in this regard the conquered might be allowed the traditional privilege of conquering the conquerors. Nietzsche answered roundly, "the German does not yet know the meaning of the word culture," and in the essay on history set himself to show that the so-called culture was a morass into which the German had been led by a sixth sense he had developed during the nineteenth century—the "historical sense": he had been brought by his spiritual teachers to believe that he was the "crown of the world-process" and that his highest duty lay in surrendering himself to it.

With Nietzsche, the historical sense became a "malady from which men suffer," the world-process an illusion, evolutionary theories a subtle excuse for inactivity. History is for the few not the many, for the man not the youth, for the great not the small—who are broken and bewildered by it. It is the lesson of remembrance, and few are strong enough to bear that lesson. History has no meaning except as the servant of life and action: and most of us can only act if we forget. This is the burden of the first essay; and turning from history to the historian he condemns the "noisy little fellows" who measure the motives of the great men of the past by their own, and use the past to justify their present.

But who are the men that can use history rightly, and for whom it is a help and not a hindrance to life? They are the great men of action and thought, the "lonely giants amid the pigmies." To them alone can the record of their great forebears be a consolation as well as a lesson. In the realm of thought, they are of the type of the ideal philosopher sketched in the second essay. To Nietzsche the only hope of the race lies in the "production of the genius," of the man who can bear the burden of the future and not be swamped by the past: he found the personal expression of such a man, for the time being, in Schopenhauer.

Schopenhauer here stands, as a personality, for all that makes for life in philosophy, against the stagnation of the professional philosopher. The last part of the essay is a fierce polemic against state-aided philosophy and the official position of the professors, who formed, and still form, the intellectual aristocracy of Germany, with a cathedral authority on all their pronouncements.

But "there has never been a eulogy on a philosopher," says Dr. Kögel, "that has had so little to say about his philosophy." The essay on Schopenhauer is of value precisely because it has nothing to do with Schopenhauer. We need not be disturbed by the thought that Nietzsche afterwards turned from him. He truly recognised that Schopenhauer was here merely a name for himself, that "not Schopenhauer as educator is in question, but his opposite, Nietzsche as educator" (*Ecce Homo*). He could regard Schopenhauer, later, as a siren that called to death; he put him among the great artists that lead down—who are worse than the bad artists that lead nowhere. "We must go further in the pessimistic logic than the denial of the will," he says in the *Götzendämmerung*; "we must deny Schopenhauer." The pessimism and denial of the will, the blank despair before suffering, were the shoals on which Nietzsche's reverence finally broke. They could not stand before the Dionysian outlook, whose pessimism sprang not from weakness but strength, and in which the joy of willing and being can even welcome suffering. In this essay we hear little of the pessimism, save as the imperfect and "all-too-human" side of Schopenhauer that actually brings us nearer to him. Later, he could part the man and his work, and speak of Schopenhauer's view as the "Evil eye." But as yet he is a young man who has kept his illusions, and, like Ogniben, he judges men by what they might be.

Afterwards, he judged himself too in these essays by "what he might be." "To me," he said in *Ecce Homo*, "they are promises: I know not what they mean to others."

It is also in the belief they are promises that they are here translated "for others." The *Thoughts out of Season* are the first announcement of the complex theme of the *Zarathustra*. They form the best possible introduction to Nietzschean thought. Nietzsche is already the knight-errant of philosophy: but his adventure is just beginning.

A. C.

THE USE AND ABUSE OF HISTORY.

PREFACE.

"I HATE everything that merely instructs me without increasing or directly quickening my activity." These words of Goethe, like a sincere *ceterum censeo*, may well stand at the head of my thoughts on the worth and the worthlessness of history. I will show in them why instruction that does not "quicken," knowledge that slackens the rein of activity, why in fact history, in Goethe's phrase, must be seriously "hated," as a costly and superfluous luxury of the understanding: for we are still in want of the necessaries of life, and the superfluous is an enemy to the necessary. We do need history, but quite differently from the jaded idlers in the garden of knowledge, however grandly they may look down on our rude and unpicturesque requirements. In other words, we need it for life and action, not as a convenient way to avoid life and action, or to excuse a selfish life and a cowardly or base action. We would serve history only so far as it serves life; but to value its study beyond a certain point mutilates and degrades life: and this is a fact that certain marked symptoms of our time make it as necessary as it may be painful to bring to the test of experience.

I have tried to describe a feeling that has often

troubled me: I revenge myself on it by giving it publicity. This may lead some one to explain to me that he has also had the feeling, but that I do not feel it purely and elementally enough, and cannot express it with the ripe certainty of experience. A few may say so ; but most people will tell me that it is a perverted, unnatural, horrible, and altogether unlawful feeling to have, and that I show myself unworthy of the great historical movement which is especially strong among the German people for the last two generations.

I am at all costs going to venture on a description of my feelings; which will be decidedly in the interests of propriety, as I shall give plenty of opportunity for paying compliments to such a "movement." And I gain an advantage for myself that is more valuable to me than propriety— the attainment of a correct point of view, through my critics, with regard to our age.

These thoughts are "out of season," because I am trying to represent something of which the age is rightly proud—its historical culture—as a fault and a defect in our time, believing as I do that we are all suffering from a malignant historical fever and should at least recognise the fact. But even if it be a virtue, Goethe may be right in asserting that we cannot help developing our faults at the same time as our virtues ; and an excess of virtue can obviously bring a nation to ruin, as well as an excess of vice. In any case I may be allowed my say. But I will first relieve my mind by the confession that the experiences which produced those disturbing feelings were mostly drawn from myself,

—and from other sources only for the sake of comparison ; and that I have only reached such "unseasonable" experience, so far as I am the nursling of older ages like the Greek, and less a child of this age.   I must admit so much in virtue of my profession as a classical scholar: for I do not know what meaning classical scholarship may have for our time except in its being "unseasonable,"—that is, contrary to our time, and yet with an influence on it for the benefit, it may be hoped, of a future time.

THE USE AND ABUSE OF HISTORY.

I.

CONSIDER the herds that are feeding yonder: they know not the meaning of yesterday or to-day; they graze and ruminate, move or rest, from morning to night, from day to day, taken up with their little loves and hates, at the mercy of the moment, feeling neither melancholy nor satiety. Man cannot see them without regret, for even in the pride of his humanity he looks enviously on the beast's happiness. He wishes simply to live without satiety or pain, like the beast; yet it is all in vain, for he will not change places with it. He may ask the beast—"Why do you look at me and not speak to me of your happiness?" The beast wants to answer—"Because I always forget what I wished to say": but he forgets this answer too, and is silent; and the man is left to wonder.

He wonders also about himself, that he cannot learn to forget, but hangs on the past: however far or fast he run, that chain runs with him. It is matter for wonder: the moment, that is here and gone, that was nothing before and nothing after, returns like a spectre to trouble the quiet of a later moment. A leaf is continually dropping out of the volume of time and fluttering away—and suddenly it flutters back into the man's lap. Then he says, "I remember . . . ," and envies the beast, that forgets at once, and sees every moment really die, sink into night and mist, extinguished for ever. The beast lives *unhistorically*; for it "goes into" the present, like a number, without leaving any curious remainder. It cannot dissimulate, it conceals nothing; at every moment it seems what it actually is, and thus can be nothing that is not honest. But man is always resisting the great and continually increasing weight of the past; it presses him down, and bows his shoulders; he travels with a dark invisible burden that he can plausibly disown, and is only too glad to disown in converse with his fellows—in order to excite their envy. And so it hurts him, like the thought of a lost Paradise, to see a herd grazing, or, nearer still, a child, that has nothing yet of the past to disown, and plays in a happy blindness between the walls of the past and the future. And yet its play must be disturbed, and only too soon will it be summoned from its little kingdom of oblivion. Then it learns to understand the words "once upon a time," the "open sesame" that lets in battle, suffering and weariness on mankind, and reminds them what their existence really is, an imperfect tense that never becomes a present. And when death brings at last the desired forgetfulness, it abolishes life and being together, and sets the seal on the knowledge that "being" is merely a continual "has been," a thing that lives by denying and destroying and contradicting itself.

If happiness and the chase for new happiness keep alive in any sense the will to live, no philosophy has perhaps more truth than the cynic's: for the beast's happiness, like that of the perfect cynic, is the visible proof of the truth of cynicism. The smallest pleasure, if it be only continuous and make one happy, is incomparably a greater happiness than the more intense pleasure that comes as an episode, a wild freak, a mad interval between ennui, desire, and privation. But in the smallest and greatest happiness there is always one thing that makes it happiness: the power of forgetting, or, in more learned phrase, the capacity of feeling "unhistorically" throughout its duration. One who cannot leave himself behind on the threshold of the moment and forget the past, who cannot stand on a single point, like a goddess of victory, without fear or giddiness, will never know what happiness is; and, worse still, will never do anything to make others happy. The extreme case would be the man without any power to forget, who is condemned to see "becoming" everywhere. Such a man believes no more in himself or his own existence, he sees everything fly past in an eternal succession, and loses himself in the stream of becoming. At last, like the logical disciple of Heraclitus, he will hardly dare to raise his finger. Forgetfulness is a property of all action; just as not only light but darkness is bound up

with the life of every organism. One who wished
to feel everything historically, would be like a man
forcing himself to refrain from sleep, or a beast
who had to live by chewing a continual cud. Thus
even a happy life is possible without remembrance,
as the beast shows: but life in any true sense is
absolutely impossible without forgetfulness. Or,
to put my conclusion better, there is a degree of
sleeplessness, of rumination, of "historical sense,"
that injures and finally destroys the living thing,
be it a man or a people or a system of culture.

To fix this degree and the limits to the memory
of the past, if it is not to become the gravedigger
of the present, we must see clearly how great is
the "plastic power" of a man or a community or
a culture; I mean the power of specifically growing
out of one's self, of making the past and the strange
one body with the near and the present, of healing
wounds, replacing what is lost, repairing broken
moulds. There are men who have this power so
slightly that a single sharp experience, a single
pain, often a little injustice, will lacerate their
souls like the scratch of a poisoned knife. There
are others, who are so little injured by the worst
misfortunes, and even by their own spiteful actions,
as to feel tolerably comfortable, with a fairly quiet
conscience, in the midst of them,—or at any rate
shortly afterwards. The deeper the roots of a
man's inner nature, the better will he take the
past into himself; and the greatest and most
powerful nature would be known by the absence
of limits for the historical sense to overgrow and
work harm. It would assimilate and digest the

past, however foreign, and turn it to sap. Such
a nature can forget what it cannot subdue; there
is no break in the horizon, and nothing to remind
it that there are still men, passions, theories and
aims on the other side. This is a universal law;
a living thing can only be healthy, strong and
productive within a certain horizon: if it be incapable of drawing one round itself, or too selfish
to lose its own view in another's, it will come to
an untimely end. Cheerfulness, a good conscience,
belief in the future, the joyful deed, all depend,
in the individual as well as the nation, on there
being a line that divides the visible and clear from
the vague and shadowy: we must know the right
time to forget as well as the right time to remember; and instinctively see when it is necessary
to feel historically, and when unhistorically. This
is the point that the reader is asked to consider;
that the unhistorical and the historical are equally
necessary to the health of an individual, a community, and a system of culture.

Every one has noticed that a man's historical
knowledge and range of feeling may be very
limited, his horizon as narrow as that of an Alpine
valley, his judgments incorrect and his experience
falsely supposed original, and yet in spite of all the
incorrectness and falsity he may stand forth in
unconquerable health and vigour, to the joy of
all who see him; whereas another man with far
more judgment and learning will fail in comparison,
because the lines of his horizon are continually
changing and shifting, and he cannot shake himself
free from the delicate network of his truth and

righteousness for a downright act of will or desire.
We saw that the beast, absolutely "unhistorical,"
with the narrowest of horizons, has yet a certain
happiness, and lives at least without hypocrisy or
ennui; and so we may hold the capacity of feeling
(to a certain extent) unhistorically, to be the more
important and elemental, as providing the foundation of every sound and real growth, everything
that is truly great and human. The unhistorical
is like the surrounding atmosphere that can alone
create life, and in whose annihilation life itself
disappears. It is true that man can only become
man by first suppressing this unhistorical element
in his thoughts, comparisons, distinctions, and conclusions, letting a clear sudden light break through
these misty clouds by his power of turning the
past to the uses of the present. But an excess of
history makes him flag again, while without the
veil of the unhistorical he would never have the
courage to begin. What deeds could man ever
have done if he had not been enveloped in the
dust-cloud of the unhistorical? Or, to leave
metaphors and take a concrete example, imagine
a man swayed and driven by a strong passion,
whether for a woman or a theory. His world is
quite altered. He is blind to everything behind
him, new sounds are muffled and meaningless;
though his perceptions were never so intimately
felt in all their colour, light and music, and he
seems to grasp them with his five senses together.
All his judgments of value are changed for the
worse; there is much he can no longer value, as
he can scarcely feel it: he wonders that he has so

long been the sport of strange words and opinions, that his recollections have run round in one un-wearying circle and are yet too weak and weary to make a single step away from it. His whole case is most indefensible; it is narrow, ungrateful to the past, blind to danger, deaf to warnings, a small living eddy in a dead sea of night and forgetfulness. And yet this condition, unhistorical and antihistorical throughout, is the cradle not only of unjust action, but of every just and justifiable action in the world. No artist will paint his picture, no general win his victory, no nation gain its freedom, without having striven and yearned for it under those very "unhistorical" conditions. If the man of action, in Goethe's phrase, is without conscience, he is also without knowledge: he forgets most things in order to do one, he is unjust to what is behind him, and only recognises one law, the law of that which is to be. So he loves his work infinitely more than it deserves to be loved; and the best works are produced in such an ecstasy of love that they must always be unworthy of it, however great their worth otherwise.

Should any one be able to dissolve the un-historical atmosphere in which every great event happens, and breathe afterwards, he might be capable of rising to the "super-historical" stand-point of consciousness, that Niebuhr has de-scribed as the possible result of historical research. "History," he says, "is useful for one purpose, if studied in detail: that men may know, as the greatest and best spirits of our generation

do not know, the accidental nature of the forms
in which they see and insist on others seeing,—
insist, I say, because their consciousness of them
is exceptionally intense.   Any one who has not
grasped this idea in its different applications will
fall under the spell of a more powerful spirit who
reads a deeper emotion into the given form."   Such
a standpoint might be called "super-historical,"
as one who took it could feel no impulse from
history to any further life or work, for he would
have recognised the blindness and injustice in the
soul of the doer as a condition of every deed: he
would be cured henceforth of taking history too
seriously, and have learnt to answer the question
how and why life should be lived,—for all men
and all circumstances, Greeks or Turks, the first
century or the nineteenth.   Whoever asks his
friends whether they would live the last ten or
twenty years over again, will easily see which of
them is born for the "super-historical standpoint":
they will all answer no, but will give different
reasons for their answer.   Some will say they
have the consolation that the next twenty will
be better: they are the men referred to satirically
by David Hume:—

" And from the dregs of life hope to receive,
  What the first sprightly running could not give."

We will call them the "historical men."   Their
vision of the past turns them towards the future,
encourages them to persevere with life, and kindles
the hope that justice will yet come and happiness
is behind the mountain they are climbing.   They

believe that the meaning of existence will become
ever clearer in the course of its evolution, they
only look backward at the process to understand
the present and stimulate their longing for the
future. They do not know how unhistorical their
thoughts and actions are in spite of all their history,
and how their preoccupation with it is for the sake
of life rather than mere science.

But that question to which we have heard the
first answer, is capable of another; also a "no,"
but on different grounds. It is the "no" of the
"super-historical" man who sees no salvation in
evolution, for whom the world is complete and
fulfils its aim in every single moment. How could
the next ten years teach what the past ten were
not able to teach?

Whether the aim of the teaching be happiness or
resignation, virtue or penance, these super-historical
men are not agreed; but as against all merely
historical ways of viewing the past, they are unani-
mous in the theory that the past and the present
are one and the same, typically alike in all their
diversity, and forming together a picture of eternally
present imperishable types of unchangeable value
and significance. Just as the hundreds of different
languages correspond to the same constant and
elemental needs of mankind, and one who understood the needs could learn nothing new from the
languages; so the "super-historical" philosopher
sees all the history of nations and individuals from
within. He has a divine insight into the original
meaning of the hieroglyphs, and comes even to be
weary of the letters that are continually unrolled

before him.   How should the endless rush of events
not bring satiety, surfeit, loathing?   So the boldest
of us is ready perhaps at last to say from his heart
with Giacomo Leopardi : " Nothing lives that were
worth thy pains, and the earth deserves not a sigh.
Our being is pain and weariness, and the world is
mud—nothing else.   Be calm."

But we will leave the super-historical men to
their loathings and their wisdom : we wish rather
to-day to be joyful in our unwisdom and have a
pleasant life as active men who go forward, and
respect the course of the world.   The value we put
on the historical may be merely a Western prejudice : let us at least go forward within this prejudice and not stand still.   If we could only learn
better to study history as a means to life !   We
would gladly grant the super-historical people their
superior wisdom, so long as we are sure of having
more life than they : for in that case our unwisdom
would have a greater future before it than their
wisdom.   To make my opposition between life and
wisdom clear, I will take the usual road of the short
summary.

A historical phenomenon, completely understood
and reduced to an item of knowledge, is, in relation
to the man who knows it, dead : for he has found
out its madness, its injustice, its blind passion, and
especially the earthly and darkened horizon that
was the source of its power for history.   This power
has now become, for him who has recognised it,
powerless ; not yet, perhaps, for him who is alive.

History regarded as pure knowledge and allowed
to sway the intellect would mean for men the final

balancing of the ledger of life. Historical study is only fruitful for the future if it follow a powerful life-giving influence, for example, a new system of culture; only, therefore, if it be guided and dominated by a higher force, and do not itself guide and dominate.

History, so far as it serves life, serves an unhistorical power, and thus will never become a pure science like mathematics. The question how far life needs such a service is one of the most serious questions affecting the well-being of a man, a people and a culture. For by excess of history life becomes maimed and degenerate, and is followed by the degeneration of history as well.

II.

The fact that life does need the service of history must be as clearly grasped as that an excess of history hurts it; this will be proved later. History is necessary to the living man in three ways: in relation to his action and struggle, his conservatism and reverence, his suffering and his desire for deliverance. These three relations answer to the three kinds of history—so far as they can be distinguished —the *monumental*, the *antiquarian*, and the *critical*.

History is necessary above all to the man of action and power who fights a great fight and needs examples, teachers and comforters; he cannot find them among his contemporaries. It was necessary in this sense to Schiller; for our time is so evil, Goethe says, that the poet meets no nature that will profit him, among living men.   Polybius is thinking of the active man when he calls political history the true preparation for governing a state; it is the great teacher, that shows us how to bear steadfastly the reverses of fortune, by reminding us of what others have suffered.   Whoever has learned to recognise this meaning in history must hate to see curious tourists and laborious beetle-hunters climbing up the great pyramids of antiquity.   He does not wish to meet the idler who is rushing through the picture-galleries of the past for a new distraction or sensation, where he himself is looking for example and encouragement.   To avoid being troubled by the weak and hopeless idlers, and those whose apparent activity is merely neurotic, he looks behind him and stays his course towards the goal in order to breathe.   His goal is happiness, not perhaps his own, but often the nation's, or humanity's at large: he avoids quietism, and uses history as a weapon against it.   For the most part he has no hope of reward except fame, which means the expectation of a niche in the temple of history, where he in his turn may be the consoler and counsellor of posterity.   For his orders are that what has once been able to extend the conception "man" and give it a fairer content, must ever exist for the same office.   The great moments in the individual battle form a chain, a high road for humanity through the ages, and the highest points of those vanished moments are yet great and living for men; and this is the fundamental idea of the belief in humanity, that finds a voice in the demand for a "monumental" history.

VOL. II.   B

But the fiercest battle is fought round the demand for greatness to be eternal. Every other living thing cries no. " Away with the monuments," is the watchword. Dull custom fills all the chambers of the world with its meanness, and rises in thick vapour round anything that is great, barring its way to immortality, blinding and stifling it. And the way passes through mortal brains! Through the brains of sick and short-lived beasts that ever rise to the surface to breathe, and painfully keep off annihilation for a little space. For they wish but one thing : to live at any cost. Who would ever dream of any " monumental history " among them, the hard torch-race that alone gives life to greatness? And yet there are always men awakening, who are strengthened and made happy by gazing on past greatness, as though man's life were a lordly thing, and the fairest fruit of this bitter tree were the knowledge that there was once a man who walked sternly and proudly through this world, another who had pity and loving-kindness, another who lived in contemplation,—but all leaving one truth behind them, that his life is the fairest who thinks least about life. The common man snatches greedily at this little span, with tragic earnestness, but they, on their way to monumental history and immortality, knew how to greet it with Olympic laughter, or at least with a lofty scorn ; and they went down to their graves in irony—for what had they to bury? Only what they had always treated as dross, refuse, and vanity, and which now falls into its true home of oblivion, after being so long the sport of their contempt. One thing will live, the sign-manual of their inmost being, the rare flash of light, the deed, the creation; because posterity cannot do without it. In this spiritualised form fame is something more than the sweetest morsel for our egoism, in Schopenhauer's phrase: it is the belief in the oneness and continuity of the great in every age, and a protest against the change and decay of generations.

What is the use to the modern man of this " monumental" contemplation of the past, this pre-occupation with the rare and classic? It is the knowledge that the great thing existed and was therefore possible, and so may be possible again. He is heartened on his way; for his doubt in weaker moments, whether his desire be not for the impossible, is struck aside. Suppose one believe that no more than a hundred men, brought up in the new spirit, efficient and productive, were needed to give the deathblow to the present fashion of education in Germany; he will gather strength from the remembrance that the culture of the Renaissance was raised on the shoulders of such another band of a hundred men.

And yet if we really wish to learn something from an example, how vague and elusive do we find the comparison! If it is to give us strength, many of the differences must be neglected, the in-dividuality of the past forced into a general formula and all the sharp angles broken off for the sake of correspondence. Ultimately, of course, what was once possible can only become possible a second time on the Pythagorean theory, that when the heavenly bodies are in the same position again, the events on earth are reproduced to the smallest detail; so when the stars have a certain relation, a Stoic and an Epicurean will form a conspiracy to murder Cæsar, and a different conjunction will show another Columbus discovering America. Only if the earth always began its drama again after the fifth act, and it were certain that the same inter-action of motives, the same *deus ex machina*, the same catastrophe would occur at particular intervals, could the man of action venture to look for the whole archetypic truth in monumental history, to see each fact fully set out in its uniqueness: it would not probably be before the astronomers became astrologers again. Till then monumental history will never be able to have complete truth ; it will always bring together things that are in-compatible and generalise them into compatibility, will always weaken the differences of motive and occasion. Its object is to depict effects at the expense of the causes—" monumentally," that is, as examples for imitation: it turns aside, as far as it may, from reasons, and might be called with far less exaggeration a collection of " effects in themselves," than of events that will have an effect on all ages. The events of war or religion cherished in our popular celebrations are such " effects in them-selves " ; it is these that will not let ambition sleep, and lie like amulets on the bolder hearts—not the real historical nexus of cause and effect, which, rightly understood, would only prove that nothing quite similar could ever be cast again from the dice-boxes of fate and the future.

As long as the soul of history is found in the

great impulse that it gives to a powerful spirit, as
long as the past is principally used as a model for
imitation, it is always in danger of being a little
altered and touched up, and brought nearer to
fiction.   Sometimes there is no possible distinction
between a " monumental" past and a mythical
romance, as the same motives for action can be
gathered from the one world as the other.   If this
monumental method of surveying the past dominate the others,—the antiquarian and the critical,—
the past itself suffers wrong.   Whole tracts of it
are forgotten and despised ; they flow away like a
dark unbroken river, with only a few gaily coloured
islands of fact rising above it.   There is something
beyond nature in the rare figures that become
visible, like the golden hips that his disciples attri-
buted to Pythagoras.   Monumental history lives
by false analogy ; it entices the brave to rashness,
and the enthusiastic to fanaticism by its tempting
comparisons.   Imagine this history in the hands—
and the head—of a gifted egoist or an inspired
scoundrel ; kingdoms will be overthrown, princes
murdered, war and revolution let loose, and the
number of " effects in themselves "—in other words,
effects without sufficient cause — increased.   So
much for the harm done by monumental history
to the powerful men of action, be they good or
bad ; but what if the weak and the inactive take it
as their servant—or their master !

Consider the simplest and commonest example,
the inartistic or half artistic natures whom a monumental history provides with sword and buckler.
They will use the weapons against their hereditary

enemies, the great artistic spirits, who alone can
learn from that history the one real lesson, how to
live, and embody what they have learnt in noble
action. Their way is obstructed, their free air
darkened by the idolatrous — and conscientious
—dance round the half understood monument of
a great past. "See, that is the true and real art,"
we seem to hear: " of what use are these aspiring
little people of to-day?" The dancing crowd has
apparently the monopoly of "good taste": for the
creator is always at a disadvantage compared with
the mere looker-on, who never put a hand to the
work; just as the arm-chair politician has ever had
more wisdom and foresight than the actual statesman. But if the custom of democratic suffrage
and numerical majorities be transferred to the
realm of art, and the artist put on his defence
before the court of æsthetic dilettanti, you may take
your oath on his condemnation; although, or rather
because, his judges had proclaimed solemnly the
canon of "monumental art," the art that has
"had an effect on all ages," according to the
official definition. In their eyes no need nor inclination nor historical authority is in favour of the
art which is not yet "monumental" because it is
contemporary. Their instinct tells them that art
can be slain by art: the monumental will never be
reproduced, and the weight of its authority is invoked
from the past to make it sure. They are connoisseurs of art, primarily because they wish to kill art;
they pretend to be physicians, when their real idea is
to dabble in poisons. They develop their tastes to
a point of perversion, that they may be able to show

a reason for continually rejecting all the nourish-
ing artistic fare that is offered them.   For they do
not want greatness, to arise : their method is to say,
" See, the great thing is already here !"   In reality
they care as little about the great thing that is
already here, as that which is about to arise : their
lives are evidence of that.   Monumental history is
the cloak under which their hatred of present power
and greatness masquerades as an extreme admira-
tion of the past : the real meaning of this way of
viewing history is disguised as its opposite ; whether
they wish it or no, they are acting as though their
motto were, " let the dead bury the—living."

Each of the three kinds of history will only
flourish in one ground and climate : otherwise it
grows to a noxious weed.   If the man who will
produce something great, have need of the past,
he makes himself its master by means of monumental history : the man who can rest content with
the traditional and venerable, uses the past as an
" antiquarian historian ": and only he whose heart
is oppressed by an instant need, and who will cast
the burden off at any price, feels the want of
" critical history," the history that judges and
condemns.   There is much harm wrought by
wrong and thoughtless planting : the critic without
the need, the antiquary without piety, the knower
of the great deed who cannot be the doer of it, are
plants that have grown to weeds, they are torn
from their native soil and therefore degenerate.

III

Secondly, history is necessary to the man of conservative and reverent nature, who looks back to the origins of his existence with love and trust; through it, he gives thanks for life. He is careful to preserve what survives from ancient days, and will reproduce the conditions of his own upbringing for those who come after him ; thus he does life a service. The possession of his ancestors' furniture changes its meaning in his soul: for his soul is rather possessed by it. All that is small and limited, mouldy and obsolete, gains a worth and inviolability of its own from the conservative and reverent soul of the antiquary migrating into it, and building a secret nest there. The history of his town becomes the history of himself; he looks on the walls, the turreted gate, the town council, the fair, as an illustrated diary of his youth, and sees himself in it all—his strength, industry, desire, reason, faults and follies. " Here one could live," he says, " as one can live here now—and will go on living; for we are tough folk, and will not be uprooted in the night." And so, with his " we," he surveys the marvellous individual life of the past and identifies himself with the spirit of the house, the family and the city. He greets the soul of his people from afar as his own, across the dim and troubled centuries: his gifts and his virtues lie in such power of feeling and divination, his scent of a half-vanished trail, his instinctive correctness in reading the scribbled past, and understanding at

once its palimpsests—nay, its polypsests.   Goethe
stood with such thoughts before the monument of
Erwin von Steinbach: the storm of his feeling rent
the historical cloud-veil that hung between them,
and he saw the German work for the first time
"coming from the stern, rough, German soul."
This was the road that the Italians of the Renaissance travelled, the spirit that reawakened the
ancient Italic genius in their poets to "a wondrous
echo of the immemorial lyre," as Jacob Burckhardt
says.   But the greatest value of this antiquarian
spirit of reverence lies in the simple emotions of
pleasure and content that it lends to the drab,
rough, even painful circumstances of a nation's or
individual's life: Niebuhr confesses that he could
live happily on a moor among free peasants with
a history, and would never feel the want of art.
How could history serve life better than by
anchoring the less gifted races and peoples to the
homes and customs of their ancestors, and keeping
them from ranging far afield in search of better,
to find only struggle and competition?   The
influence that ties men down to the same companions and circumstances, to the daily round of
toil, to their bare mountain-side,—seems to be
selfish and unreasonable: but it is a healthy
unreason and of profit to the community; as
every one knows who has clearly realised the
terrible consequences of mere desire for migration
and adventure,—perhaps in whole peoples,—or who
watches the destiny of a nation that has lost confidence in its earlier days, and is given up to a
restless cosmopolitanism and an unceasing desire

for novelty. The feeling of the tree that clings to its roots, the happiness of knowing one's growth to be not merely arbitrary and fortuitous, but the inheritance, the fruit and blossom of a past, that does not merely justify but crown the present—this is what we nowadays prefer to call the real historical sense.

These are not the conditions most favourable to reducing the past to pure science: and we see here too, as we saw in the case of monumental history, that the past itself suffers when history serves life and is directed by its end. To vary the metaphor, the tree feels its roots better than it can see them: the greatness of the feeling is measured by the greatness and strength of the visible branches. The tree may be wrong here; how far more wrong will it be in regard to the whole forest, which it only knows and feels so far as it is hindered or helped by it, and not otherwise! The antiquarian sense of a man, a city or a nation has always a very limited field. Many things are not noticed at all; the others are seen in isolation, as through a microscope. There is no measure: equal importance is given to everything, and therefore too much to anything. For the things of the past are never viewed in their true perspective or receive their just value; but value and perspective change with the individual or the nation that is looking back on its past.

There is always the danger here, that everything ancient will be regarded as equally venerable, and everything without this respect for antiquity, like a new spirit, rejected as an enemy. The Greeks themselves admitted the archaic style of plastic art by the side of the freer and greater style; and later, did not merely tolerate the pointed nose and the cold mouth, but made them even a canon of taste. If the judgment of a people harden in this way, and history's service to the past life be to undermine a further and higher life; if the historical sense no longer preserve life, but mummify it: then the tree dies, unnaturally, from the top downwards, and at last the roots themselves wither. Antiquarian history degenerates from the moment that it no longer gives a soul and inspiration to the fresh life of the present. The spring of piety is dried up, but the learned habit persists without it and revolves complaisantly round its own centre. The horrid spectacle is seen of the mad collector raking over all the dust-heaps of the past. He breathes a mouldy air; the antiquarian habit may degrade a considerable talent, a real spiritual need in him, to a mere insatiable curiosity for everything old: he often sinks so low as to be satisfied with any food, and greedily devour all the scraps that fall from the bibliographical table.

Even if this degeneration do not take place, and the foundation be not withered on which antiquarian history can alone take root with profit to life: yet there are dangers enough, if it become too powerful and invade the territories of the other methods. It only understands how to preserve life, not to create it; and thus always undervalues the present growth, having, unlike monumental history, no certain instinct for it. Thus it hinders the mighty impulse to a new deed and paralyses the doer, who must always, as doer, be grazing some piety or other. The fact that has grown old carries with it a demand for its own immortality. For when one considers the life-history of such an ancient fact, the amount of reverence paid to it for generations—whether it be a custom, a religious creed, or a political principle,—it seems presumptuous, even impious, to replace it by a new fact, and the ancient congregation of pieties by a new piety.

Here we see clearly how necessary a third way of looking at the past is to man, beside the other two. This is the "critical" way; which is also in the service of life. Man must have the strength to break up the past; and apply it too, in order to live. He must bring the past to the bar of judgment, interrogate it remorselessly, and finally condemn it. Every past is worth condemning: this is the rule in mortal affairs, which always contain a large measure of human power and human weakness. It is not justice that sits in judgment here; nor mercy that proclaims the verdict; but only life, the dim, driving force that insatiably desires—itself. Its sentence is always unmerciful, always unjust, as it never flows from a pure fountain of knowledge: though it would generally turn out the same, if Justice herself delivered it. "For everything that is born is *worthy* of being destroyed: better were it then that nothing should be born." It requires great strength to be able to live and forget how far life and injustice are one. Luther himself once said that the world only arose by an oversight of

God; if he had ever dreamed of heavy ordnance, he would never have created it. The same life that needs forgetfulness, needs sometimes its destruction; for should the injustice of something ever become obvious—a monopoly, a caste, a dynasty for example—the thing deserves to fall. Its past is critically examined, the knife put to its roots, and all the "pieties" are grimly trodden under foot. The process is always dangerous, even for life; and the men or the times that serve life in this way, by judging and annihilating the past, are always dangerous to themselves and others. For as we are merely the resultant of previous generations, we are also the resultant of their errors, passions, and crimes: it is impossible to shake off this chain. Though we condemn the errors and think we have escaped them, we cannot escape the fact that we spring from them. At best, it comes to a conflict between our innate, inherited nature and our knowledge, between a stern, new discipline and an ancient tradition; and we plant a new way of life, a new instinct, a second nature, that withers the first. It is an attempt to gain a past *a posteriori* from which we might spring, as against that from which we do spring; always a dangerous attempt, as it is difficult to find a limit to the denial of the past, and the second natures are generally weaker than the first. We stop too often at knowing the good without doing it, because we also know the better but cannot do it. Here and there the victory is won, which gives a strange consolation to the fighters, to those who use critical history for the sake of life. The consolation is the knowledge that this "first nature" was once a second, and that every conquering "second nature" becomes a first.

IV.

This is how history can serve life. Every man and nation needs a certain knowledge of the past, whether it be through monumental, antiquarian, or critical history, according to his objects, powers, and necessities. The need is not that of the mere thinkers who only look on at life, or the few who desire knowledge and can only be satisfied with knowledge; but it has always a reference to the end of life, and is under its absolute rule and direction. This is the natural relation of an age, a culture and a people to history; hunger is its source, necessity its norm, the inner plastic power assigns its limits. The knowledge of the past is only desired for the service of the future and the present, not to weaken the present or undermine a living future. All this is as simple as truth itself, and quite convincing to any one who is not in the toils of "historical deduction."

And now to take a quick glance at our time! We fly back in astonishment. The clearness, naturalness, and purity of the connection between life and history has vanished; and in what a maze of exaggeration and contradiction do we now see the problem! Is the guilt ours who see it, or have life and history really altered their conjunction and an inauspicious star risen between them?

Others may prove we have seen falsely; I am merely saying what we believe we see. There is such a star, a bright and lordly star, and the conjunction is really altered—by science, and the demand for history to be a science. Life is no more dominant, and knowledge of the past no longer its thrall: boundary marks are overthrown and everything bursts its limits. The perspective of events is blurred, and the blur extends through their whole immeasurable course. No generation has seen such a panoramic comedy as is shown by the " science of universal evolution," history; that shows it with the dangerous audacity of its motto— " Fiat veritas, pereat vita."

Let me give a picture of the spiritual events in the soul of the modern man. Historical knowledge streams on him from sources that are inexhaustible, strange incoherencies come together, memory opens all its gates and yet is never open wide enough, nature busies herself to receive all the foreign guests, to honour them and put them in their places. But they are at war with each other: violent measures seem necessary, in order to escape destruction one's self. It becomes second nature to grow gradually accustomed to this irregular and stormy home-life, though this second nature is unquestionably weaker, more restless, more radically unsound than the first. The modern man carries inside him an enormous heap of indigestible knowledge-stones that occasionally rattle together in his body, as the fairy-tale has it. And the rattle reveals the most striking characteristic of these modern men, the opposition of something inside them to which nothing external corresponds ; and the reverse. The ancient nations knew nothing of this. Knowledge, taken in excess without hunger, even contrary to desire, has no more the effect of transforming the external life ; and remains hidden in a chaotic inner world that the modern man has a curious pride in calling his "real personality." He has the substance, he says, and only wants the form ; but this is quite an unreal opposition in a living thing. Our modern culture is for that reason not a living one, because it cannot be understood without that opposition. In other words, it is not a real culture but a kind of knowledge about culture, a complex of various thoughts and feelings about it, from which no decision as to its direction can come. Its real motive force that issues in visible action is often no more than a mere convention, a wretched imitation, or even a shameless caricature. The man probably feels like the snake that has swallowed a rabbit whole and lies still in the sun, avoiding all movement not absolutely necessary. The "inner life" is now the only thing that matters to education, and all who see it hope that the education may not fail by being too indigestible. Imagine a Greek meeting it ; he would observe that for modern men "education" and "historical education" seem to mean the same thing, with the difference that the one phrase is longer. And if he spoke of his own theory, that a man can be very well educated without any history at all, people would shake their heads and think they had not heard aright. The Greeks, the famous people of a past still near to us, had the "unhistorical sense" strongly developed in the period of their greatest power. If a typical child of his age were transported to that world by some enchantment, he would probably find the Greeks very "uneducated." And that discovery would betray the closely guarded secret of modern culture to the laughter of the world. For we moderns have nothing of our own. We only become worth notice by filling ourselves to overflowing with foreign customs, arts, philosophies, religions and sciences: we are wandering encyclopædias, as an ancient Greek who had strayed into our time would probably call us. But the only value of an encyclopædia lies in the inside, in the contents, not in what is written outside, in the binding or the wrapper. And so the whole of modern culture is essentially internal; the bookbinder prints something like this on the cover: "Manual of internal culture for external barbarians." The opposition of inner and outer makes the outer side still more barbarous, as it would naturally be, when the outward growth of a rude people merely developed its primitive inner needs. For what means has nature of repressing too great a luxuriance from without? Only one,—to be affected by it as little as possible, to set it aside and stamp it out at the first opportunity. And so we have the custom of no longer taking real things seriously, we get the feeble personality on which the real and the permanent make so little impression. Men become at last more careless and accommodating in external matters, and the

considerable cleft between substance and form is
widened; until they have no longer any feeling for
barbarism, if only their memories be kept continually titillated, and there flow a constant stream
of new things to be known, that can be neatly
packed up in the cupboards of their memory.
The culture of a people as against this barbarism,
can be, I think, described with justice as the
"unity of artistic style in every outward expression of the people's life." This must not be misunderstood, as though it were merely a question
of the opposition between barbarism and "fine
style." The people that can be called cultured,
must be in a real sense a living unity, and not be
miserably cleft asunder into form and substance.
If one wish to promote a people's culture, let him
try to promote this higher unity first, and work
for the destruction of the modern educative system
for the sake of a true education. Let him dare to
consider how the health of a people that has been
destroyed by history may be restored, and how it
may recover its instincts with its honour.

I am only speaking, directly, about the Germans
of the present day, who have had to suffer more
than other people from the feebleness of personality
and the opposition of substance and form. " Form "
generally implies for us some convention, disguise
or hypocrisy, and if not hated, is at any rate not
loved. We have an extraordinary fear of both the
word convention and the thing. This fear drove
the German from the French school; for he wished
to become more natural, and therefore more German.
But he seems to have come to a false conclusion

with his " therefore." First he ran away from his
school of convention, and went by any road he
liked : he has come ultimately to imitate voluntarily
in a slovenly fashion, what he imitated painfully
and often successfully before. So now the lazy
fellow lives under French conventions that are
actually incorrect : his manner of walking shows it,
his conversation and dress, his general way of life.
In the belief that he was returning to Nature, he
merely followed caprice and comfort, with the
smallest possible amount of self-control. Go
through any German town ; you will see conventions that are nothing but the negative aspect of
the national characteristics of foreign states. Everything is colourless, worn out, shoddy and ill-copied.
Every one acts at his own sweet will—which is not
a strong or serious will—on laws dictated by the
universal rush and the general desire for comfort.
A dress that made no head ache in its inventing
and wasted no time in the making, borrowed from
foreign models and imperfectly copied, is regarded
as an important contribution to German fashion.
The sense of form is ironically disclaimed by the
people—for they have the " sense of substance " :
they are famous for their cult of " inwardness."

But there is also a famous danger in their " inwardness " : the internal substance cannot be
seen from the outside, and so may one day take
the opportunity of vanishing, and no one notice its
absence, any more than its presence before. One
may think the German people to be very far from
this danger : yet the foreigner will have some
warrant for his reproach that our inward life is too

weak and ill-organised to provide a form and
external expression for itself. It may in rare cases
show itself finely receptive, earnest and powerful,
richer perhaps than the inward life of other peoples :
but, taken as a whole, it remains weak, as all its
fine threads are not tied together in one strong
knot. The visible action is not the self-manifes-
tation of the inward life, but only a weak and crude
attempt of a single thread to make a show of
representing the whole. And thus the German is
not to be judged on any one action, for the individual may be as completely obscure after it as
before. He must obviously be measured by his
thoughts and feelings, which are now expressed in
his books; if only the books did not, more than
ever, raise the doubt whether the famous inward
life is still really sitting in its inaccessible shrine.
It might one day vanish and leave behind it only
the external life,—with its vulgar pride and vain
servility,—to mark the German. Fearful thought!
—as fearful as if the inward life still sat there,
painted and rouged and disguised, become a play-
actress or something worse; as his theatrical
experience seems to have taught the quiet observer
Grillparzer, standing aside as he did from the
main press. "We feel by theory," he says. "We
hardly know any more how our contemporaries
give expression to their feelings : we make them use
gestures that are impossible nowadays. Shakespeare has spoilt us moderns."

This is a single example, its general application
perhaps too hastily assumed. But how terrible it
would be were that generalisation justified before

our eyes ! There would be then a note of despair in
the phrase, " We Germans feel by theory, we are
all spoilt by history ; "—a phrase that would cut
at the roots of any hope for a future national
culture. For every hope of that kind grows from
the belief in the genuineness and immediacy of
German feeling, from the belief in an untarnished
inward life. Where is our hope or belief, when its
spring is muddied, and the inward quality has
learned gestures and dances and the use of cosmetics,
has learned to express itself " with due reflection in
abstract terms," and gradually to lose itself? And
how should a great productive spirit exist among
a nation that is not sure of its inward unity and is
divided into educated men whose inner life has
been drawn from the true path of education, and
uneducated men whose inner life cannot be ap-
proached at all? How should it exist, I say, when
the people has lost its own unity of feeling, and knows
that the feeling of the part calling itself the educated
part and claiming the right of controlling the
artistic spirit of the nation, is false and hypocritical?
Here and there the judgment and taste of individuals may be higher and finer than the rest, but
that is no compensation : it tortures a man to have
to speak only to one section and be no longer in
sympathy with his people. He would rather bury
his treasure now, in disgust at the vulgar patronage
of a class, though his heart be filled with tenderness
for all. The instinct of the people can no longer
meet him half-way; it is useless for them to stretch
their arms out to him in yearning. What remains
but to turn his quickened hatred against the ban,

strike at the barrier raised by the so-called culture, and condemn as judge what blasted and degraded him as a living man and a source of life? He takes a profound insight into fate in exchange for the godlike desire of creation and help, and ends his days as a lonely philosopher, with the wisdom of disillusion. It is the painfullest comedy: he who sees it will feel a sacred obligation on him, and say to himself,—" Help must come: the higher unity in the nature and soul of a people must be brought back, the cleft between inner and outer must again disappear under the hammer of necessity." But to what means can he look? What remains to him now but his knowledge? He hopes to plant the feeling of a need, by speaking from the breadth of that knowledge, giving it freely with both hands. From the strong need the strong action may one day arise. And to leave no doubt of the instance I am taking of the need and the knowledge, my testimony shall stand, that it is German unity in its highest sense which is the goal of our endeavour, far more than political union: it is the unity of the German spirit and life after the annihilation of the antagonism between form and substance, inward life and convention

V.

An excess of history seems to be an enemy to the life of a time, and dangerous in five ways. Firstly, the contrast of inner and outer is emphasised and personality weakened. Secondly, the time comes to imagine that it possesses the rarest

of virtues, justice, to a higher degree than any
other time.   Thirdly, the instincts of a nation are
thwarted, the maturity of the individual arrested
no less than that of the whole.   Fourthly, we get
the belief in the old age of mankind, the belief, at
all times harmful, that we are late survivals, mere
Epigoni.   Lastly, an age reaches a dangerous condition of irony with regard to itself, and the still
more dangerous state of cynicism, when a cunning
egoistic theory of action is matured that maims and
at last destroys the vital strength.

To return to the first point: the modern man
suffers from a weakened personality.   The Roman
of the Empire ceased to be a Roman through the
contemplation of the world that lay at his feet; he
lost himself in the crowd of foreigners that streamed
into Rome, and degenerated amid the cosmopolitan
carnival of arts, worships and moralities.   It is the
same with the modern man, who is continually
having a world-panorama unrolled before his eyes
by his historical artists.   He is turned into a
restless, dilettante spectator, and arrives at a condition when even great wars and revolutions cannot
affect him beyond the moment.   The war is hardly
at an end, and it is already converted into thousands
of copies of printed matter, and will be soon served
up as the latest means of tickling the jaded palates
of the historical gourmets.   It seems impossible for
a strong full chord to be prolonged, however
powerfully the strings are swept: it dies away
again the next moment in the soft and strength-
less echo of history.   In ethical language, one never
succeeds in staying on a height; your deeds are

sudden crashes, and not a long roll of thunder. One may bring the greatest and most marvellous thing to perfection; it must yet go down to Orcus unhonoured and unsung. For art flies away when you are roofing your deeds with the historical awning. The man who wishes to understand everything in a moment, when he ought to grasp the unintelligible as the sublime by a long struggle, can be called intelligent only in the sense of Schiller's epigram on the "reason of reasonable men." There is something the child sees that he does not see; something the child hears that he does not hear; and this something is the most important thing of all. Because he does not understand it, his understanding is more childish than the child's and more simple than simplicity itself; in spite of the many clever wrinkles on his parchment face, and the masterly play of his fingers in unravelling the knots. He has lost or destroyed his instinct; he can no longer trust the "divine animal" and let the reins hang loose, when his understanding fails him and his way lies through the desert. His individuality is shaken, and left without any sure belief in itself; it sinks into its own inner being, which only means here the disordered chaos of what it has learned, which will never express itself externally, being mere dogma that cannot turn to life. Looking further, we see how the banishment of instinct by history has turned men to shades and abstractions: no one ventures to show a personality, but masks himself as a man of culture, a savant, poet or politician. If one take hold of these masks, believing he has to do with a serious thing and not a mere puppet-show—for they all have an appearance of seriousness—he will find nothing but rags and coloured streamers in his hands. He must deceive himself no more, but cry aloud, " Off with your jackets, or be what you seem!" A man of the royal stock of seriousness must no longer be a Don Quixote, for he has better things to do than to tilt at such pretended realities. But he must always keep a sharp look about him, call his " Halt! who goes there?" to all the shrouded figures, and tear the masks from their faces. And see the result! One might have thought that history encouraged men above all to be honest, even if it were only to be honest fools : this used to be its effect, but is so no longer. Historical education and the uniform frock-coat of the citizen are both dominant at the same time. While there has never been such a full-throated chatter about " free personality," personalities can be seen no more (to say nothing of free ones); but merely men in uniform, with their coats anxiously pulled over their ears. Individuality has withdrawn itself to its recesses; it is seen no more from the outside, which makes one doubt if it be possible to have causes without effects. Or will a race of eunuchs prove to be necessary to guard the historical harem of the world? We can understand the reason for their aloofness very well. Does it not seem as if their task were to watch over history to see that nothing comes out except other histories, but no deed that might be historical; to prevent personalities becoming " free," that is, sincere towards themselves and others, both in word and deed? Only through this sincerity will the inner need and misery of the modern man be brought to the light, and art and religion come as true helpers in the place of that sad hypocrisy of convention and masquerade, to plant a common culture which will answer to real necessities, and not teach, as the present " liberal education " teaches, to tell lies about these needs, and thus become a walking lie one's self.

In such an age, that suffers from its "liberal education," how unnatural, artificial and unworthy will be the conditions under which the sincerest of all sciences, the holy naked goddess Philosophy, must exist! She remains, in such a world of compulsion and outward conformity, the subject of the deep monologue of the lonely wanderer or the chance prey of any hunter, the dark secret of the chamber or the daily talk of the old men and children at the university. No one dare fulfil the law of philosophy in himself; no one lives philosophically, with that single-hearted virile faith that forced one of the olden time to bear himself as a Stoic, wherever he was and whatever he did, if he had once sworn allegiance to the Stoa. All modern philosophising is political or official, bound down to be a mere phantasmagoria of learning by our modern governments, churches, universities, moralities and cowardices: it lives by sighing "if only . . ." and by knowing that "it happened once upon a time. . . ." Philosophy has no place in historical education, if it will be more than the knowledge that lives indoors, and can have no expression in action.   Were the modern man once courageous and determined, and not merely such an indoor being even in his hatreds, he would banish philosophy.   At present he is satisfied with modestly covering her nakedness.   Yes, men think, write, print, speak and teach philosophically: so much is permitted them.   It is only otherwise in action, in "life."   Only one thing is permitted there, and everything else quite impossible: such are the orders of historical education. " Are these human beings," one might ask, " or only machines for thinking, writing and speaking ? "

Goethe says of Shakespeare : " No one has more despised correctness of costume than he : he knows too well the inner costume that all men wear alike. You hear that he describes Romans wonderfully ; I do not think so : they are flesh - and - blood Englishmen ; but at any rate they are men from top to toe, and the Roman toga sits well on them." Would it be possible, I wonder, to represent our present literary and national heroes, officials and politicians as Romans?   I am sure it would not, as they are no men, but incarnate compendia, abstractions made concrete.   If they have a character of their own, it is so deeply sunk that it can never rise to the light of day : if they are men, they are only men to a physiologist.   To all others they are something else, not men, not " beasts or gods," but historical pictures of the march of civilisation, and nothing but pictures and civilisation, form without any ascertainable substance, bad form unfortunately, and uniform at that.   And in this way my thesis is to be understood and con-

sidered : " only strong personalities can endure
history, the weak are extinguished by it." History
unsettles the feelings when they are not powerful
enough to measure the past by themselves. The
man who dare no longer trust himself, but asks
history against his will for advice " how he ought
to feel now," is insensibly turned by his timidity
into a play-actor, and plays a part, or generally
many parts,—very badly therefore and superficially.
Gradually all connection ceases between the man
and his historical subjects. We see noisy little
fellows measuring themselves with the Romans
as though they were like them : they burrow in
the remains of the Greek poets, as if these
were *corpora* for their dissection — and as *vilia*
as their own well - educated *corpora* might be.
Suppose a man is working at Democritus. The
question is always on my tongue, why precisely
Democritus? Why not Heraclitus, or Philo, or
Bacon, or Descartes? And then, why a philosopher? Why not a poet or orator? And why
especially a Greek? Why not an Englishman
or a Turk? Is not the past large enough to let
you find some place where you may disport your-
self without becoming ridiculous? But, as I said,
they are a race of eunuchs : and to the eunuch one
woman is the same as another, merely a woman,
" woman in herself," the Ever - unapproachable.
And it is indifferent what they study, if history
itself always remain beautifully "objective" to
them, as men, in fact, who could never make history
themselves. And since the Eternal Feminine
could never " draw you upward," you draw it down

to you, and being neuter yourselves, regard history
as neuter also.   But in order that no one may take
my comparison of history and the Eternal Feminine
too seriously, I will say at once that I hold it, on
the contrary, to be the Eternal Masculine : I only
add that for those who are " historically trained "
throughout, it must be quite indifferent which it is ;
for they are themselves neither man nor woman,
nor even hermaphrodite, but mere neuters, or, in
more philosophic language, the Eternal Objective.

If the personality be once emptied of its sub-
jectivity, and come to what men call an " objective "
condition, nothing can have any more effect on
it.   Something good and true may be done, in
action, poetry or music : but the hollow culture of
the day will look beyond the work and ask the
history of the author.   If the author have already
created something, our historian will set out clearly
the past and the probable future course of his
development, he will put him with others and
compare them, and separate by analysis the choice
of his material and his treatment ; he will wisely
sum the author up and give him general advice for
his future path.   The most astonishing works may
be created ; the swarm of historical neuters will
always be in their place, ready to consider the
author through their long telescopes.   The echo is
heard at once : but always in the form of " criticism," though the critic never dreamed of the work's
possibility a moment before.   It never comes to
have an influence, but only a criticism : and the
criticism itself has no influence, but only breeds
another criticism.   And so we come to consider

the fact of many critics as a mark of influence, that of few or none as a mark of failure. Actually everything remains in the old condition, even in the presence of such "influence": men talk a little while of a new thing, and then of some other new thing, and in the meantime they do what they have always done. The historical training of our critics prevents their having an influence in the true sense, an influence on life and action. They put their blotting paper on the blackest writing, and their thick brushes over the gracefullest designs; these they call "corrections";—and that is all. Their critical pens never cease to fly, for they have lost power over them; they are driven by their pens instead of driving them. The weakness of modern personality comes out well in the measureless overflow of criticism, in the want of self-mastery, and in what the Romans called *impotentia.*

VI.

But leaving these weaklings, let us turn rather to a point of strength for which the modern man is famous. Let us ask the painful question whether he has the right in virtue of his historical "objectivity" to call himself strong and just in a higher degree than the man of another age. Is it true that this objectivity has its source in a heightened sense of the need for justice? Or, being really an effect of quite other causes, does it only have the appearance of coming from justice, and really lead to an unhealthy prejudice in favour

of the modern man? Socrates thought it near
madness to imagine one possessed a virtue without really possessing it. Such imagination has
certainly more danger in it than the contrary
madness of a positive vice. For of this there is
still a cure; but the other makes a man or a time
daily worse, and therefore more unjust.

No one has a higher claim to our reverence than
the man with the feeling and the strength for
justice. For the highest and rarest virtues unite
and are lost in it, as an unfathomable sea absorbs
the streams that flow from every side. The hand
of the just man, who is called to sit in judgment,
trembles no more when it holds the scales: he
piles the weights inexorably against his own side,
his eyes are not dimmed as the balance rises and
falls, and his voice is neither hard nor broken when
he pronounces the sentence. Were he a cold
demon of knowledge, he would cast round him the
icy atmosphere of an awful, superhuman majesty,
that we should fear, not reverence. But he is a
man, and has tried to rise from a careless doubt to
a strong certainty, from a gentle tolerance to the
imperative "thou must"; from the rare virtue of
magnanimity to the rarest, of justice. He has
come to be like that demon without being more
than a poor mortal at the outset; above all, he has
to atone to himself for his humanity and tragically
shatter his own nature on the rock of an impossible
virtue.—All this places him on a lonely height as
the most reverend example of the human race.
For truth is his aim, not in the form of cold
ineffectual knowledge, but the truth of the judge

who punishes according to law ; not as the selfish possession of an individual, but the sacred authority that removes the boundary stones from all selfish possessions ; truth, in a word, as the tribunal of the world, and not as the chance prey of a single hunter. The search for truth is often thoughtlessly praised : but it only has anything great in it if the seeker have the sincere unconditional will for justice. Its roots are in justice alone : but a whole crowd of different motives may combine in the search for it, that have nothing to do with truth at all ; curiosity, for example, or dread of ennui, envy, vanity, or amusement. Thus the world seems to be full of men who "serve truth" : and yet the virtue of justice is seldom present, more seldom known, and almost always mortally hated. On the other hand a throng of sham virtues has entered in at all times with pomp and honour.

Few in truth serve truth, as only few have the pure will for justice ; and very few even of these have the strength to be just. The will alone is not enough : the impulse to justice without the power of judgment has been the cause of the greatest suffering to men. And thus the common good could require nothing better than for the seed of this power to be strewn as widely as possible, that the fanatic may be distinguished from the true judge, and the blind desire from the conscious power. But there are no means of planting a power of judgment : and so when one speaks to men of truth and justice, they will be ever troubled by the doubt whether it be the fanatic or the judge who is speaking to them. And they must be pardoned for always treating the "servants of truth" with special kindness, who possess neither the will nor the power to judge and have set before them the task of finding "pure knowledge without reference to consequences," knowledge, in plain terms, that comes to nothing. There are very many truths which are unimportant; problems that require no struggle to solve, to say nothing of sacrifice. And in this safe realm of indifference a man may very successfully become a "cold demon of knowledge." And yet—if we find whole regiments of learned inquirers being turned to such demons in some age specially favourable to them, it is always unfortunately possible that the age is lacking in a great and strong sense of justice, the noblest spring of the so-called impulse to truth.

Consider the historical virtuoso of the present time: is he the justest man of his age? True, he has developed in himself such a delicacy and sensitiveness that "nothing human is alien to him." Times and persons most widely separated come together in the concords of his lyre. He has become a passive instrument, whose tones find an echo in similar instruments: until the whole atmosphere of a time is filled with such echoes, all buzzing in one soft chord. Yet I think one only hears the overtones of the original historical note: its rough powerful quality can be no longer guessed from these thin and shrill vibrations. The original note sang of action, need, and terror; the overtone lulls us into a soft dilettante sleep. It is as though the heroic symphony had been arranged for two flutes for the use of dreaming opium-smokers. We

can now judge how these virtuosi stand towards the
claim of the modern man to a higher and purer conception of justice. This virtue has never a pleasing
quality; it never charms; it is harsh and strident.
Generosity stands very low on the ladder of the
virtues in comparison; and generosity is the mark
of a few rare historians! Most of them only get as
far as tolerance, in other words they leave what
cannot be explained away, they correct it and
touch it up condescendingly, on the tacit assump-
tion that the novice will count it as justice if the
past be narrated without harshness or open expressions of hatred. But only superior strength can
really judge; weakness must tolerate, if it do not
pretend to be strength and turn justice to a play-
actress. There is still a dreadful class of historians
remaining—clever, stern and honest, but narrow-
minded: who have the "good will" to be just with
a pathetic belief in their actual judgments, which
are all false; for the same reason, almost, as the
verdicts of the usual juries are false. How difficult
it is to find a real historical talent, if we exclude
all the disguised egoists, and the partisans who
pretend to take up an impartial attitude for the
sake of their own unholy game! And we also
exclude the thoughtless folk who write history in
the naïve faith that justice resides in the popular
view of their time, and that to write in the spirit of
the time is to be just; a faith that is found in all
religions, and which, in religion, serves very well.
The measurement of the opinions and deeds of the
past by the universal opinions of the present is
called "objectivity" by these simple people: they

find the canon of all truth here: their work is to adapt the past to the present triviality. And they call all historical writing "subjective" that does not regard these popular opinions as canonical.

Might not an illusion lurk in the highest interpretation of the word objectivity? We understand by it a certain standpoint in the historian, who sees the procession of motive and consequence too clearly for it to have an effect on his own personality. We think of the æsthetic phenomenon of the detachment from all personal concern with which the painter sees the picture and forgets himself, in a stormy landscape, amid thunder and lightning, or on a rough sea: and we require the same artistic vision and absorption in his object from the historian. But it is only a superstition to say that the picture given to such a man by the object really shows the truth of things. Unless it be that objects are expected in such moments to paint or photograph themselves by their own activity on a purely passive medium!

But this would be a myth, and a bad one at that. One forgets that this moment is actually the powerful and spontaneous moment of creation in the artist, of "composition" in its highest form, of which the result will be an artistically, but not an historically, true picture. To think objectively, in this sense, of history is the work of the dramatist: to think one thing with another, and weave the elements into a single whole; with the presumption that the unity of plan must be put into the objects if it be not already there. So man veils and subdues the past, and expresses his impulse to art—

but not his impulse to truth or justice. Objectivity and justice have nothing to do with each other. There could be a kind of historical writing that had no drop of common fact in it and yet could claim to be called in the highest degree objective. Grillparzer goes so far as to say that " history is nothing but the manner in which the spirit of man apprehends facts that are obscure to him, links things together whose connection heaven only knows, replaces the unintelligible by something intelligible, puts his own ideas of causation into the external world, which can perhaps be explained only from within : and assumes the existence of chance, where thousands of small causes may be really at work. Each man has his own individual needs, and so millions of tendencies are running together, straight or crooked, parallel or across, forward or backward, helping or hindering each other. They have all the appearance of chance, and make it impossible, quite apart from all natural influences, to establish any universal lines on which past events must have run." But as a result of this so-called " objective " way of looking at things, such a " must " ought to be made clear. It is a presumption that takes a curious form if adopted by the historian as a dogma. Schiller is quite clear about its truly subjective nature when he says of the historian, " one event after the other begins to draw away from blind chance and lawless freedom, and take its place as the member of an harmonious whole—*which is of course only apparent in its presentation.*" But what is one to think of the innocent statement, wavering between tautology and nonsense, of a famous historical virtuoso? "It seems that all human actions and impulses are subordinate to the process of the material world, that works unnoticed, powerfully and irresistibly." In such a sentence one no longer finds obscure wisdom in the form of obvious folly; as in the saying of Goethe's gardener, "Nature may be forced but not compelled," or in the notice on the side-show at a fair, in Swift: "The largest elephant in the world, except himself, to be seen here." For what opposition is there between human action and the process of the world? It seems to me that such historians cease to be instructive as soon as they begin to generalise; their weakness is shown by their obscurity. In other sciences the generalisations are the most important things, as they contain the laws. But if such generalisations as these are to stand as laws, the historian's labour is lost; for the residue of truth, after the obscure and insoluble part is removed, is nothing but the commonest knowledge. The smallest range of experience will teach it. But to worry whole peoples for the purpose, and spend many hard years of work on it, is like crowding one scientific experiment on another long after the law can be deduced from the results already obtained: and this absurd excess of experiment has been the bane of all natural science since Zöllner. If the value of a drama lay merely in its final scene, the drama itself would be a very long, crooked and laborious road to the goal: and I hope history will not find its whole significance in general propositions, and regard them as its blossom and fruit. On the contrary, its real value lies in inventing ingenious variations on a probably commonplace theme, in raising the popular melody to a universal symbol and showing what a world of depth, power and beauty exists in it.

But this requires above all a great artistic faculty, a creative vision from a height, the loving study of the data of experience, the free elaborating of a given type,—objectivity in fact, though this time as a positive quality. Objectivity is so often merely a phrase. Instead of the quiet gaze of the artist that is lit by an inward flame, we have an affectation of tranquillity; just as a cold detachment may mask a lack of moral feeling. In some cases a triviality of thought, the everyday wisdom that is too dull not to seem calm and disinterested, comes to represent the artistic condition in which the subjective side has quite sunk out of sight. Everything is favoured that does not rouse emotion, and the driest phrase is the correct one. They go so far as to accept a man who is *not affected at all* by some particular moment in the past as the right man to describe it. This is the usual relation of the Greeks and the classical scholars. They have nothing to do with each other—and this is called "objectivity"! The intentional air of detachment that is assumed for effect, the sober art of the superficial motive-hunter is most exasperating when the highest and rarest things are in question; and it is the *vanity* of the historian that drives him to this attitude of indifference. He goes to justify the axiom that a man's vanity corresponds to his lack of wit. No, be honest at any rate! Do not pretend to the artist's strength, that is the real objectivity;

do not try to be just, if you are not born to that dread vocation. As if it were the task of every time to be just to everything before it! Ages and generations have never the right to be the judges of all previous ages and generations: only to the rarest men in them can that difficult mission fall. Who compels you to judge? If it is your wish— you must prove first that you are capable of justice. As judges, you must stand higher than that which is to be judged : as it is, you have only come later. The guests that come last to the table should rightly take the last places: and will you take the first? Then do some great and mighty deed : the place may be prepared for you then, even though you do come last.

You can only explain the past by what is highest in the present. Only by straining the noblest qualities you have to their highest power will you find out what is greatest in the past, most worth knowing and preserving. Like by like! otherwise you will draw the past to your own level. Do not believe any history that does not spring from the mind of a rare spirit. You will know the quality of the spirit, by its being forced to say something universal, or to repeat something that is known already ; the fine historian must have the power of coining the known into a thing never heard before and proclaiming the universal so simply and profoundly that the simple is lost in the profound, and the profound in the simple. No one can be a great historian and artist, and a shallowpate at the same time. But one must not despise the workers who sift and cast together the material because they can never become great historians. They must, still less, be confounded with them, for they are the necessary bricklayers and apprentices in the service of the master: just as the French used to speak, more naïvely than a German would, of the "historiens de M. Thiers." These workmen should gradually become extremely learned, but never, for that reason, turn to be masters. Great learning and great shallowness go together very well under one hat.

Thus, history is to be written by the man of experience and character. He who has not lived through something greater and nobler than others, will not be able to explain anything great and noble in the past. The language of the past is always oracular: you will only understand it as builders of the future who know the present. We can only explain the extraordinarily wide influence of Delphi by the fact that the Delphic priests had an exact knowledge of the past: and, similarly, only he who is building up the future has a right to judge the past. If you set a great aim before your eyes, you control at the same time the itch for analysis that makes the present into a desert for you, and all rest, all peaceful growth and ripening, impossible. Hedge yourselves with a great, all-embracing hope, and strive on. Make of yourselves a mirror where the future may see itself, and forget the superstition that you are Epigoni. You have enough to ponder and find out, in pondering the life of the future: but do not ask history to show you the means and the instrument to it. If you live yourselves back into the history of great men, you will find in it the high command to come to maturity and leave that blighting system of cultivation offered by your time: which sees its own profit in not allowing you to become ripe, that it may use and dominate you while you are yet unripe. And if you want biographies, do not look for those with the legend "Mr. So-and-so and his times," but for one whose title-page might be inscribed "a fighter against his time." Feast your souls on Plutarch, and dare to believe in yourselves when you believe in his heroes. A hundred such men—educated against the fashion of to-day, made familiar with the heroic, and come to maturity—are enough to give an eternal quietus to the noisy sham education of this time.

VII.

The unrestrained historical sense, pushed to its logical extreme, uproots the future, because it destroys illusions and robs existing things of the only atmosphere in which they can live. Historical justice, even if practised conscientiously, with a pure heart, is therefore a dreadful virtue, because it always undermines and ruins the living thing: its judgment always means annihilation. If there be no constructive impulse behind the historical one, if the clearance of rubbish be not merely to leave the ground free for the hopeful living future to build its house, if justice alone be supreme, the creative instinct is sapped and discouraged. A religion, for example, that has to be turned into a matter of historical knowledge by the power of

pure justice, and to be scientifically studied
throughout, is destroyed at the end of it all. For
the historical audit brings so much to light which
is false and absurd, violent and inhuman, that the
condition of pious illusion falls to pieces. And a
thing can only live through a pious illusion. For
man is creative only through love and in the
shadow of love's illusions, only through the unconditional belief in perfection and righteousness.
Everything that forces a man to be no longer un-
conditioned in his love, cuts at the root of his
strength: he must wither, and be dishonoured.
Art has the opposite effect to history: and only
perhaps if history suffer transformation into a pure
work of art, can it preserve instincts or arouse
them. Such history would be quite against the
analytical and inartistic tendencies of our time, and
even be considered false. But the history that
merely destroys without any impulse to construct,
will in the long-run make its instruments tired of
life; for such men destroy illusions, and "he who
destroys illusions in himself and others is punished
by the ultimate tyrant, Nature." For a time a man
can take up history like any other study, and it
will be perfectly harmless. Recent theology seems
to have entered quite innocently into partnership
with history, and scarcely sees even now that it has
unwittingly bound itself to the Voltairean *écrasez*!
No one need expect from that any new and powerful constructive impulse: they might as well have
let the so-called Protestant Union serve as the
cradle of a new religion, and the jurist Holtzendorf,
the editor of the far more dubiously named Pro-

testant Bible, be its John the Baptist. This state
of innocence may be continued for some time by
the Hegelian philosophy,—still seething in some
of the older heads,—by which men can distinguish
the "idea of Christianity" from its various imperfect
"manifestations"; and persuade themselves that it
is the "self-movement of the Idea" that is ever
particularising itself in purer and purer forms, and
at last becomes the purest, most transparent, in
fact scarcely visible form in the brain of the present
theologus liberalis vulgaris. But to listen to this
pure Christianity speaking its mind about the
earlier impure Christianity, the uninitiated hearer
would often get the impression that the talk was
not of Christianity at all but of . . .—what are we
to think? if we find Christianity described by the
"greatest theologians of the century" as the religion that claims to "find itself in all real religions
and some other barely possible religions," and
if the "true church" is to be a thing "which
may become a liquid mass with no fixed outline,
with no fixed place for its different parts, but everything to be peacefully welded together"—what, I
ask again, are we to think?

Christianity has been denaturalised by historical
treatment—which in its most complete form means
"just" treatment—until it has been resolved into
pure knowledge and destroyed in the process.
This can be studied in everything that has life.
For it ceases to have life if it be perfectly dissected,
and lives in pain and anguish as soon as the
historical dissection begins. There are some who
believe in the saving power of German music to

revolutionise the German nature. They angrily exclaim against the special injustice done to our culture, when such men as Mozart and Beethoven are beginning to be spattered with the learned mud of the biographers and forced to answer a thousand searching questions on the rack of historical criticism. Is it not premature death, or at least mutilation, for anything whose living influence is not yet exhausted, when men turn their curious eyes to the little minutiæ of life and art, and look for problems of knowledge where one ought to learn to live, and forget problems? Set a couple of these modern biographers to consider the origins of Christianity or the Lutheran reformation : their sober, practical investigations would be quite sufficient to make all spiritual "action at a distance" impossible : just as the smallest animal can prevent the growth of the mightiest oak by simply eating up the acorn. All living things need an atmosphere, a mysterious mist, around them. If that veil be taken away and a religion, an art, or a genius condemned to revolve like a star without an atmosphere, we must not be surprised if it becomes hard and unfruitful, and soon withers. It is so with all great things "that never prosper without some illusion," as Hans Sachs says in the Meistersinger.

Every people, every man even, who would become ripe, needs such a veil of illusion, such a protecting cloud. But now men hate to become ripe, for they honour history above life. They cry in triumph that "science is now beginning to rule life." Possibly it might ; but a life thus ruled is

not of much value. It is not such true *life*, and
promises much less for the future than the life that
used to be guided not by science, but by instincts
and powerful illusions. But this is not to be the
age of ripe, alert and harmonious personalities, but
of work that may be of most use to the commonwealth. Men are to be fashioned to the needs of
the time, that they may soon take their place in
the machine. They must work in the factory of
the " common good " before they are ripe, or rather
to prevent them becoming ripe ; for this would
be a luxury that would draw away a deal of power
from the " labour market." Some birds are blinded
that they may sing better ; I do not think men
sing to-day better than their grandfathers, though
I am sure they are blinded early. But light, too
clear, too sudden and dazzling, is the infamous
means used to blind them. The young man is
kicked through all the centuries : boys who know
nothing of war, diplomacy, or commerce are considered fit to be introduced to political history.
We moderns also run through art galleries and
hear concerts in the same way as the young man
runs through history. We can feel that one thing
sounds differently from another, and pronounce on
the different " effects." And the power of gradually
losing all feelings of strangeness or astonishment,
and finally being pleased at anything, is called the
historical sense, or historical culture. The crowd
of influences streaming on the young soul is so
great, the clods of barbarism and violence flung at
him so strange and overwhelming, that an assumed
stupidity is his only refuge. Where there is a

subtler and stronger self-consciousness we find
another emotion too—disgust. The young man
has become homeless: he doubts all ideas, all
moralities. He knows "it was different in every
age, and what you are does not matter." In a
heavy apathy he lets opinion on opinion pass by
him, and understands the meaning of Hölderlin's
words when he read the work of Diogenes Laertius
on the lives and doctrines of the Greek philosophers: "I have seen here too what has often
occurred to me, that the change and waste in
men's thoughts and systems is far more tragic
than the fates that overtake what men are accustomed to call the only realities." No, such study
of history bewilders and overwhelms. It is not
necessary for youth, as the ancients show, but even
in the highest degree dangerous, as the moderns
show. Consider the historical student, the heir of
ennui, that appears even in his boyhood. He has
the "methods" for original work, the "correct
ideas" and the airs of the master at his fingers'
ends. A little isolated period of the past is marked
out for sacrifice. He cleverly applies his method,
and produces something, or rather, in prouder
phrase, "creates" something. He becomes a
"servant of truth" and a ruler in the great domain
of history. If he was what they call ripe as a
boy, he is now over-ripe. You only need shake
him and wisdom will rattle down into your lap;
but the wisdom is rotten, and every apple has its
worm. Believe me, if men work in the factory of
science and have to make themselves useful before
they are really ripe, science is ruined as much as

the slaves who have been employed too soon. I am sorry to use the common jargon about slave-owners and taskmasters in respect of such conditions, that might be thought free from any economic taint: but the words "factory, labour-market, auction-sale, practical use," and all the auxiliaries of egoism, come involuntarily to the lips in describing the younger generation of savants. Successful mediocrity tends to become still more mediocre, science still more "useful." Our modern savants are only wise on one subject, in all the rest they are, to say the least, different from those of the old stamp. In spite of that they demand honour and profit for themselves, as if the state and public opinion were bound to take the new coinage for the same value as the old. The carters have made a trade-compact among themselves, and settled that genius is superfluous, for every carrier is being re-stamped as one. And probably a later age will see that their edifices are only carted together and not built. To those who have ever on their lips the modern cry of battle and sacrifice—"Division of labour! fall into line!" we may say roundly: "If you try to further the progress of science as quickly as possible, you will end by destroying it as quickly as possible; just as the hen is worn out which you force to lay too many eggs." The progress of science has been amazingly rapid in the last decade; but consider the savants, those exhausted hens. They are certainly not "harmonious" natures: they can merely cackle more than before, because they lay eggs oftener: but the eggs are always smaller,

though their books are bigger.   The natural result
of it all is the favourite "popularising" of science
(or rather its feminising and infantising), the
villainous habit of cutting the cloth of science to
fit the figure of the "general public."   Goethe saw
the abuse in this, and demanded that science
should only influence the outer world by way of
a nobler ideal of action.   The older generation
of savants had good reason for thinking this abuse
an oppressive burden: the modern savants have an
equally good reason for welcoming it, because,
leaving their little corner of knowledge out of
account, they are part of the "general public"
themselves, and its needs are theirs.   They only
require to take themselves less seriously to be able
to open their little kingdom successfully to popular
curiosity.   This easy-going behaviour is called "the
modest condescension of the savant to the people";
whereas in reality he has only "descended" to
himself, so far as he is not a savant but a plebeian.
Rise to the conception of a people, you learned
men; you can never have one noble or high
enough.   If you thought much of the people, you
would have compassion towards them, and shrink
from offering your historical aquafortis as a refresh-
ing drink.   But you really think very little of them,
for you dare not take any reasonable pains for their
future; and you act like practical pessimists, men
who feel the coming catastrophe and become indifferent and careless of their own and others'
existence.   "If only the earth last for us: and if
it do not last, it is no matter."   Thus they come
to live an *ironical* existence.

VIII.

It may seem a paradox, though it is none, that I should attribute a kind of "ironical self-consciousness" to an age that is generally so honestly, and clamorously, vain of its historical training; and should see a suspicion hovering near it that there is really nothing to be proud of, and a fear lest the time for rejoicing at historical knowledge may soon have gone by. Goethe has shown a similar riddle in man's nature, in his remarkable study of Newton: he finds a "troubled feeling of his own error" at the base—or rather on the height —of his being, just as if he was conscious at times of having a deeper insight into things, that vanished the moment after. This gave him a certain ironical view of his own nature. And one finds that the greater and more developed "historical men" are conscious of all the superstition and absurdity in the belief that a people's education need be so extremely historical as it is; the mightiest nations, mightiest in action and influence, have lived otherwise, and their youth has been trained otherwise. The knowledge gives a sceptical turn to their minds. "The absurdity and superstition," these sceptics say, "suit men like ourselves, who come as the latest withered shoots of a gladder and mightier stock, and fulfil Hesiod's prophecy, that men will one day be born gray-headed, and that Zeus will destroy that generation as soon as the sign be visible." Historical culture is really a kind of inherited grayness, and those who have borne its mark from childhood must believe instinctively in *the old age of mankind*. To old age belongs the old man's business of looking back and casting up his accounts, of seeking consolation in the memories of the past,—in historical culture. But the human race is tough and persistent, and will not admit that the lapse of a thousand years, or a hundred thousand, entitles any one to sum up its progress from the past to the future; that is, it will not be observed as a whole at all by that infinitesimal atom, the individual man. What is there in a couple of thousand years—the period of thirty-four consecutive human lives of sixty years each—to make us speak of youth at the beginning, and " the old age of mankind " at the end of them? Does not this paralysing belief in a fast-fading humanity cover the misunderstanding of a theological idea, inherited from the Middle Ages, that the end of the world is approaching and we are waiting anxiously for the judgment? Does not the increasing demand for historical judgment give us that idea in a new dress? as if our time were the latest possible time, and commanded to hold that universal judgment of the past, which the Christian never expected from a man, but from " the Son of Man." The *memento mori*, spoken to humanity as well as the individual, was a sting that never ceased to pain, the crown of mediæval knowledge and consciousness.

The opposite message of a later time, *memento vivere*, is spoken rather timidly, without the full power of the lungs ; and there is something almost dishonest about it. For mankind still keeps to

its *memento mori,* and shows it by the universal
need for history; science may flap its wings as it
will, it has never been able to gain the free air.
A deep feeling of hopelessness has remained, and
taken the historical colouring that has now darkened
and depressed all higher education. A religion
that, of all the hours of man's life, thinks the last
the most important, that has prophesied the end
of earthly life and condemned all creatures to live
in the fifth act of a tragedy, may call forth the
subtlest and noblest powers of man, but it is an
enemy to all new planting, to all bold attempts or
free aspirations. It opposes all flight into the
unknown, because it has no life or hope there
itself. It only lets the new bud press forth on
sufferance, to blight it in its own good time: "it
might lead life astray and give it a false value."
What the Florentines did under the influence of
Savonarola's exhortations, when they made the
famous holocaust of pictures, manuscripts, masks
and mirrors, Christianity would like to do with
every culture that allured to further effort and
bore that *memento vivere* on its standard. And
if it cannot take the direct way—the way of main
force—it gains its end all the same by allying
itself with historical culture, though generally
without its connivance; and speaking through its
mouth, turns away every fresh birth with a shrug
of its shoulders, and makes us feel all the more
that we are late-comers and Epigoni, that we are,
in a word, born with gray hair. The deep and
serious contemplation of the unworthiness of all
past action, of the world ripe for judgment, has

been whittled down to the sceptical consciousness that it is anyhow a good thing to know all that has happened, as it is too late to do anything better. The historical sense makes its servants passive and retrospective. Only in moments of forgetfulness, when that sense is dormant, does the man who is sick of the historical fever ever act; though he only analyses his deed again after it is over (which prevents it from having any further consequences), and finally puts it on the dissecting table for the purposes of history. In this sense we are still living in the Middle Ages, and history is still a disguised theology; just as the reverence with which the unlearned layman looks on the learned class is inherited through the clergy. What men gave formerly to the Church they give now, though in smaller measure, to science. But the fact of giving at all is the work of the Church, not of the modern spirit, which among its other good qualities has something of the miser in it, and is a bad hand at the excellent virtue of liberality.

These words may not be very acceptable, any more than my derivation of the excess of history from the mediæval *memento mori* and the hopelessness that Christianity bears in its heart towards all future ages of earthly existence. But you should always try to replace my hesitating explanations by a better one. For the origin of historical culture, and of its absolutely radical antagonism to the spirit of a new time and a "modern consciousness," must itself be known by a historical process. History must solve the

problem of history, science must turn its sting
against itself. This threefold "must" is the imperative of the "new spirit," if it is really to contain something new, powerful, vital and original.
Or is it true that we Germans—to leave the
Romance nations out of account—must always be
mere "followers" in all the higher reaches of
culture, because that is all we *can* be? The words
of Wilhelm Wackernagel are well worth pondering:
"We Germans are a nation of 'followers,' and with
all our higher science and even our faith, are
merely the successors of the ancient world. Even
those who are opposed to it are continually
breathing the immortal spirit of classical culture
with that of Christianity: and if any one could
separate these two elements from the living air
surrounding the soul of man, there would not be
much remaining for a spiritual life to exist on."
Even if we would rest content with our vocation to
follow antiquity, even if we decided to take it in an
earnest and strenuous spirit and to show our high
prerogative in our earnestness,—we should yet be
compelled to ask whether it were our eternal
destiny to be pupils of a fading antiquity. We
might be allowed at some time to put our aim
higher and further above us. And after con-
gratulating ourselves on having brought that
secondary spirit of Alexandrian culture in us to
such marvellous productiveness — through our
"universal history"—we might go on to place
before us, as our noblest prize, the still higher task
of striving beyond and above this Alexandrian
world; and bravely find our prototypes in the

ancient Greek world, where all was great, natural and human. But it is just *there* that we find the reality of a true unhistorical culture—and in spite of that, or perhaps because of it, an unspeakably rich and vital culture. Were we Germans nothing but followers, we could not be anything greater or prouder than the lineal inheritors and followers of such a culture.

This however must be added. The thought of being Epigoni, that is often a torture, can yet create a spring of hope for the future, to the individual as well as the people: so far, that is, as we can regard ourselves as the heirs and followers of the marvellous classical power, and see therein both our honour and our spur. But not as the late and bitter fruit of a powerful stock, giving that stock a further spell of cold life, as antiquaries and grave-diggers. Such late-comers live truly an ironical existence. Annihilation follows their halting walk on tiptoe through life. They shudder before it in the midst of their rejoicing over the past. They are living memories, and their own memories have no meaning; for there are none to inherit them. And thus they are wrapped in the melancholy thought that their life is an injustice, which no future life can set right again.

Suppose that these antiquaries, these late arrivals, were to change their painful ironic modesty for a certain shamelessness. Suppose we heard them saying, aloud, "The race is at its zenith, for it has manifested itself consciously for the first time." We should have a comedy, in which the dark meaning of a certain very celebrated philosophy would unroll itself for the benefit of German culture. I believe there has been no dangerous turning-point in the progress of German culture in this century that has not been made more dangerous by the enormous and still living influence of this Hegelian philosophy. The belief that one is a late-comer in the world is, anyhow, harmful and degrading: but it must appear frightful and devastating when it raises our late-comer to godhead, by a neat turn of the wheel, as the true meaning and object of all past creation, and his conscious misery is set up as the perfection of the world's history. Such a point of view has accustomed the Germans to talk of a "world-process," and justify their own time as its necessary result. And it has put history in the place of the other spiritual powers, art and religion, as the one sovereign; inasmuch as it is the "Idea realising itself," the "Dialectic of the spirit of the nations," and the "tribunal of the world."

History understood in this Hegelian way has been contemptuously called God's sojourn upon earth,—though the God was first created by the history. He, at any rate, became transparent and intelligible inside Hegelian skulls, and has risen through all the dialectically possible steps in his being up to the manifestation of the Self: so that for Hegel the highest and final stage of the world-process came together in his own Berlin existence. He ought to have said that everything after him was merely to be regarded as the musical coda of the great historical rondo,—or rather, as simply superfluous. He has not said it; and thus he has

implanted in a generation leavened throughout by
him the worship of the "power of history," that
practically turns every moment into a sheer gaping
at success, into an idolatry of the actual : for which
we have now discovered the characteristic phrase
"to adapt ourselves to circumstances."   But the
man who has once learnt to crook the knee and
bow the head before the power of history, nods
"yes" at last, like a Chinese doll, to every power,
whether it be a government or a public opinion or
a numerical majority ; and his limbs move correctly
as the power pulls the string.   If each success
have come by a "rational necessity," and every
event show the victory of logic or the "Idea,"
then—down on your knees quickly, and let every
step in the ladder of success have its reverence!
There are no more living mythologies, you say?
Religions are at their last gasp?   Look at the
religion of the power of history, and the priests of
the mythology of Ideas, with their scarred knees!
Do not all the virtues follow in the train of the new
faith?   And shall we not call it unselfishness,
when the historical man lets himself be turned into
an "objective" mirror of all that is?   Is it not
magnanimity to renounce all power in heaven and
earth in order to adore the mere fact of power?
Is it not justice, always to hold the balance of forces
in your hands and observe which is the stronger
and heavier?   And what a school of politeness is
such a contemplation of the past!   To take everything objectively, to be angry at nothing, to love
nothing, to understand everything—makes one
gentle and pliable.   Even if a man brought up in

this school will show himself openly offended, one is just as pleased, knowing it is only meant in the artistic sense of *ira et studium*, though it is really *sine ira et studio*.

What old-fashioned thoughts I have on such a combination of virtue and mythology! But they must out, however one may laugh at them. I would even say that history always teaches—"it was once," and morality—"it ought not to be, or have been." So history becomes a compendium of actual immorality. But how wrong would one be to regard history as the judge of this actual immorality! Morality is offended by the fact that a Raphael had to die at thirty-six; such a being ought not to die. If you came to the help of history, as the apologists of the actual, you would say: "he had spoken everything that was in him to speak, a longer life would only have enabled him to create a similar beauty, and not a new beauty," and so on. Thus you become an *advocatus diaboli* by setting up the success, the fact, as your idol: whereas the fact is always dull, at all times more like a calf than a god. Your apologies for history are helped by ignorance: for it is only because you do not know what a *natura naturans* like Raphael is, that you are not on fire when you think it existed once and can never exist again. Some one has lately tried to tell us that Goethe had out-lived himself with his eighty-two years: and yet I would gladly take two of Goethe's "outlived" years in exchange for whole cartloads of fresh modern lifetimes, to have another set of such conversations as those with Eckermann, and be preserved from all the "modern" talk of these esquires of the moment. How few living men have a right to live, as against those mighty dead! That the many live and those few live no longer, is simply a brutal truth, that is, a piece of unalterable folly, a blank wall of "it was once so" against the moral judgment "it ought not to have been." Yes, against the moral judgment! For you may speak of what virtue you will, of justice, courage, magnanimity, of wisdom and human compassion, —you will find the virtuous man will always rise against the blind force of facts, the tyranny of the actual, and submit himself to laws that are not the fickle laws of history. He ever swims against the waves of history, either by fighting his passions, as the nearest brute facts of his existence, or by training himself to honesty amid the glittering nets spun round him by falsehood. Were history nothing more than the "all-embracing system of passion and error," man would have to read it as Goethe wished Werther to be read;—just as if it called to him, "Be a man and follow me not!" But fortunately history also keeps alive for us the memory of the great "fighters against history," that is, against the blind power of the actual; it puts itself in the pillory just by glorifying the true historical nature in men who troubled themselves very little about the "thus it is," in order that they might follow a "thus it must be" with greater joy and greater pride. Not to drag their generation to the grave, but to found a new one—that is the motive that ever drives them onward; and even if they are born late, there is a way of living by

which they can forget it—and future generations
will know them only as the first-comers.

IX.

Is perhaps our time such a " first-comer " ?   Its
historical sense is so strong, and has such universal
and boundless expression, that future times will
commend it, if only for this, as a first-comer—
if there be any future time, in the sense of future
culture.   But here comes a grave doubt.   Close to
the modern man's pride there stands his irony
about himself, his consciousness that he must live
in a historical, or twilit, atmosphere, the fear that
he can retain none of his youthful hopes and powers.
Here and there one goes further into cynicism, and
justifies the course of history, nay, the whole
evolution of the world, as simply leading up to the
modern man, according to the cynical canon:—
" what you see now had to come, man had to be
thus and not otherwise, no one can stand against
this necessity."   He who cannot rest in a state of
irony flies for refuge to the cynicism.   The last
decade makes him a present of one of its most
beautiful inventions, a full and well-rounded phrase
for this cynicism : he calls his way of living thoughtlessly and after the fashion of his time, " the full
surrender of his personality to the world-process."
The personality and the world-process !   The world-
process and the personality of the earthworm !   If
only one did not eternally hear the word " world,
world, world," that hyperbole of all hyperboles;

when we should only speak, in a decent manner, of " man, man, man " !   Heirs of the Greeks and Romans, of Christianity ?   All that seems nothing to the cynics.   But " heirs of the world-process " ; the final target of the world-process ; the meaning and solution of all riddles of the universe, the ripest fruit on the tree of knowledge !—that is what I call a right noble thought : by this token are the first-lings of every time to be known, although they may have arrived last.   The historical imagination has never flown so far, even in a dream ; for now the history of man is merely the continuation of that of animals and plants : the universal historian finds traces of himself even in the utter depths of the sea, in the living slime.   He stands astounded in face of the enormous way that man has run, and his gaze quivers before the mightier wonder, the modern man who can see all this way !   He stands proudly on the pyramid of the world-process : and while he lays the final stone of his knowledge, he seems to cry aloud to listening Nature : " We are at the top, we are the top, we are the comple-tion of Nature ! "

O thou too proud European of the nineteenth century, art thou not mad ?   Thy knowledge does not complete Nature, it only kills thine own nature ! Measure the height of what thou knowest by the depths of thy power to *do*.   Thou climbest the sunbeams of knowledge up towards heaven—but also down to Chaos.   Thy manner of going is fatal to thee ; the ground slips from under thy feet into the unknown ; thy life has no other stay, but only spider's webs that every new stroke of thy

knowledge tears asunder.—But not another serious
word about this, for there is a lighter side to it all.

The moralist, the artist, the saint and the statesman, may well be troubled, when they see that all
foundations are breaking up in mad unconscious
ruin, and resolving themselves into the ever flowing
stream of becoming; that all creation is being
tirelessly spun into webs of history by the modern
man, the great spider in the mesh of the world-net.
We ourselves may be glad for once in a way that
we see it all in the shining magic mirror of a
philosophical parodist, in whose brain the time has
come to an ironical consciousness of itself, to a point
even of wickedness, in Goethe's phrase.   Hegel
once said, "when the spirit makes a fresh start,
we philosophers are at hand."   Our time did make
a fresh start—into irony, and lo! Edward von
Hartmann was at hand, with his famous Philosophy
of the Unconscious—or, more plainly, his philosophy of unconscious irony.   We have seldom read
a more jovial production, a greater philosophical
joke than Hartmann's book.   Any one whom it does
not fully enlighten about "becoming," who is not
swept and garnished throughout by it, is ready
to become a monument of the past himself.   The
beginning and end of the world-process, from the
first throb of consciousness to its final leap into
nothingness, with the task of our generation settled
for it;—all drawn from that clever fount of inspiration, the Unconscious, and glittering in Apocalyptic
light, imitating an honest seriousness to the life,
as if it were a serious philosophy and not a huge
joke,—such a system shows its creator to be one

of the first philosophical parodists of all time.
Let us then sacrifice on his altar, and offer the
inventor of a true universal medicine a lock of
hair, in Schleiermacher's phrase. For what
medicine would be more salutary to combat the
excess of historical culture than Hartmann's
parody of the world's history?

If we wished to express in the fewest words
what Hartmann really has to tell us from his
mephitic tripod of unconscious irony, it would be
something like this: our time could only remain
as it is, if men should become thoroughly sick of
this existence. And I fervently believe he is right.
The frightful petrifaction of the time, the restless
rattle of the ghostly bones, held naïvely up to us
by David Strauss as the most beautiful fact of all—
is justified by Hartmann not only from the past,
ex causis efficientibus, but also from the future,
ex causa finali. The rogue let light stream over
our time from the last day, and saw that it
was very good,—for him, that is, who wishes
to feel the indigestibility of life at its full
strength, and for whom the last day cannot
come quickly enough. True, Hartmann calls the
old age of life that mankind is approaching the
" old age of man ": but that is the blessed state,
according to him, where there is only a successful
mediocrity ; where art is the " evening's amusement of the Berlin financier," and " the time has
no more need for geniuses, either because it would
be casting pearls before swine, or because the time
has advanced beyond the stage where the geniuses
are found, to one more important," to that stage

of social evolution, in fact, in which every worker
"leads a comfortable existence, with hours of work
that leave him sufficient leisure to cultivate his
intellect." Rogue of rogues, you say well what is
the aspiration of present-day mankind: but you
know too what a spectre of disgust will arise at the
end of this old age of mankind, as the result of the
intellectual culture of stolid mediocrity. It is very
pitiful to see, but it will be still more pitiful yet.
"Antichrist is visibly extending his arms:" yet it
must be so, for after all we are on the right road—
of disgust at all existence. "Forward then, boldly,
with the world-process, as workers in the vineyard
of the Lord, for it is the process alone that can
lead to redemption!"

The vineyard of the Lord! The process! To
redemption! Who does not see and hear in this
how historical culture, that only knows the word
"becoming," parodies itself on purpose and says
the most irresponsible things about itself through
its grotesque mask? For what does the rogue
mean by this cry to the workers in the vineyard?
By what "work" are they to strive boldly forward?
Or, to ask another question:—what further has the
historically educated fanatic of the world-process
to do,—swimming and drowning as he is in the
sea of becoming,—that he may at last gather in
that vintage of disgust, the precious grape of the
vineyard? He has nothing to do but to live on
as he has lived, love what he has loved, hate what
he has hated, and read the newspapers he has
always read. The only sin is for him to live otherwise than he has lived. We are told how he has

lived, with monumental clearness, by that famous
page with its large typed sentences, on which the
whole rabble of our modern cultured folk have
thrown themselves in blind ecstasy, because they
believe they read their own justification there,
haloed with an Apocalyptic light.   For the unconscious parodist has demanded of every one of them,
" the full surrender of his personality to the world-
process, for the sake of his end, the redemption of
the world ": or still more clearly,—" the assertion of
the will to live is proclaimed to be the first step on
the right road: for it is only in the full surrender
to life and its sorrow, and not in the cowardice of
personal renunciation and retreat, that anything
can be done for the world-process. . . . The striving
for the denial of the individual will is as foolish as it
is useless, more foolish even than suicide. . . .
The thoughtful reader will understand without
further explanation how a practical philosophy can
be erected on these principles, and that such a
philosophy cannot endure any disunion, but only
the fullest reconciliation with life."

The thoughtful reader will understand !   Then
one really could misunderstand Hartmann !   And
what a splendid joke it is, that he should be misunderstood !   Why should the Germans of to-day be
particularly subtle ?   A valiant Englishman looks
in vain for " delicacy of perception " and dares to
say that " in the German mind there does seem to
be something splay, something blunt-edged, un-
handy and infelicitous."   Could the great German
parodist contradict this ?   According to him, we are
approaching " that ideal condition in which the

human race makes its history with full consciousness ": but we are obviously far from the perhaps more ideal condition, in which mankind can read Hartmann's book with full consciousness. If we once reach it, the word " world-process " will never pass any man's lips again without a smile. For he will remember the time when people listened to the mock gospel of Hartmann, sucked it in, attacked it, reverenced it, extended it and canonised it with all the honesty of that " German mind," with " the uncanny seriousness of an owl," as Goethe has it. But the world must go forward, the ideal condition cannot be won by dreaming, it must be fought and wrestled for, and the way to redemption lies only through joyousness, the way to redemption from that dull, owlish seriousness. The time will come when we shall wisely keep away from all constructions of the world-process, or even of the history of man ; a time when we shall no more look at masses but at individuals, who form a sort of bridge over the wan stream of becoming. They may not perhaps continue a process, but they live out of time, as contemporaries : and thanks to history that permits such a company, they live as the Republic of geniuses of which Schopenhauer speaks. One giant calls to the other across the waste spaces of time, and the high spirit-talk goes on, undisturbed by the wanton noisy dwarfs who creep among them. The task of history is to be the mediator between these, and even to give the motive and power to produce the great man. The aim of mankind can lie ultimately only in its highest examples.

Our low comedian has his word on this too with

VOL. II.   F

his wonderful dialectic, which is just as genuine
as its admirers are admirable.   " The idea of
evolution cannot stand with our giving the
world-process an endless duration in the past,
for thus every conceivable evolution must have
taken place, which is not the case (O rogue !) ; and
so we cannot allow the process an endless duration
in the future.   Both would raise the conception of
evolution to a mere ideal (And again rogue !), and
would make the world-process like the sieve of the
Danaides.   The complete victory of the logical over
the illogical (O thou complete rogue !) must coin-
cide with the last day, the end in time of the world-
process."   No, thou clear, scornful spirit, so long as
the illogical rules as it does to-day,—so long, for
example, as the world-process can be spoken of as
thou speakest of it, amid such deep-throated assent,
—the last day is yet far off.   For it is still too joyful on this earth, many an illusion still blooms here
—like the illusion of thy contemporaries about thee.
We are not yet ripe to be hurled into thy nothingness : for we believe that we shall have a still more
splendid time, when men once begin to understand
thee, thou misunderstood, unconscious one !   But
if, in spite of that, disgust shall come throned in
power, as thou hast prophesied to thy readers if
thy portrayal of the present and the future shall
prove to be right,—and no one has despised them
with such loathing as thou,—I am ready then to cry
with the majority in the form prescribed by thee,
that next Saturday evening, punctually at twelve
o'clock, thy world shall fall to pieces.   And our
decree shall conclude thus—from to-morrow time

shall not exist, and the *Times* shall no more be published. Perhaps it will be in vain, and our decree of no avail: at any rate we have still time for a fine experiment. Take a balance and put Hartmann's " Unconscious " in one of the scales, and his " World-process " in the other. There are some who believe they weigh equally; for in each scale there is an evil word—and a good joke.

When they are once understood, no one will take Hartmann's words on the world-process as anything but a joke. It is, as a fact, high time to move forward with the whole battalion of satire and malice against the excesses of the " historical sense," the wanton love of the world-process at the expense of life and existence, the blind confusion of all perspective. And it will be to the credit of the philosopher of the Unconscious that he has been the first to see the humour of the world-process, and to succeed in making others see it still more strongly by the extraordinary seriousness of his presentation. The existence of the " world " and " humanity " need not trouble us for some time, except to provide us with a good joke: for the presumption of the small earthworm is the most uproariously comic thing on the face of the earth. Ask thyself to what end thou art here, as an individual; and if no one can tell thee, try then to justify the meaning of thy existence *a posteriori*, by putting before thyself a high and noble end. Perish on that rock! I know no better aim for life than to be broken on something great and impossible, *animæ magnæ prodigus*. But if we have the doctrines of the finality of " becoming," of the flux of all ideas, types, and species, of the lack of all radical difference between man and beast (a true but fatal idea as I think),—if we have these thrust on the people in the usual mad way for another generation, no one need be surprised if that people drown on its little miserable shoals of egoism, and petrify in its self-seeking. At first it will fall asunder and cease to be a people. In its place perhaps individualist systems, secret societies for the extermination of non-members, and similar utilitarian creations, will appear on the theatre of the future. Are we to continue to work for these creations and write history from the standpoint of the *masses*; to look for laws in it, to be deduced from the needs of the masses, the laws of motion of the lowest loam and clay strata of society? The masses seem to be worth notice in three aspects only : first as the copies of great men, printed on bad paper from worn-out plates, next as a contrast to the great men, and lastly as their tools : for the rest, let the devil and statistics fly away with them ! How could statistics prove that there are laws in history?   Laws?   Yes, they may prove how common and abominably uniform the masses are : and should we call the effects of leaden folly, imitation, love and hunger—laws?   We may admit it : but we are sure of this too—that so far as there are laws in history, the laws are of no value and the history of no value either.   And least valuable of all is that kind of history which takes the great popular movements as the most important events of the past, and regards the great men only as their clearest expression, the visible bubbles on the stream.

Thus the masses have to produce the great man, chaos to bring forth order ; and finally all the hymns are naturally sung to the teeming chaos. Everything is called "great" that has moved the masses for some long time, and becomes, as they say, a "historical power." But is not this really an intentional confusion of quantity and quality? When the brutish mob have found some idea, a religious idea for example, which satisfies them, when they have defended it through thick and thin for centuries ; then, and then only, will they discover its inventor to have been a great man. The highest and noblest does not affect the masses at all. The historical consequences of Christianity, its "historical power," toughness and persistence prove nothing, fortunately, as to its founder's greatness. They would have been a witness against him. For between him and the historical success of Christianity lies a dark heavy weight of passion and error, lust of power and honour, and the crushing force of the Roman Empire. From this, Christianity had its earthly taste, and its earthly foundations too, that made its continuance in this world possible. Greatness should not depend on success ; Demosthenes is great without it. The purest and noblest adherents of Christianity have always doubted and hindered, rather than helped, its effect in the world, its so-called "historical power"; for they were accustomed to stand outside the "world," and cared little for the "process of the Christian Idea." Hence they have generally remained unknown to history, and their very names are lost. In Christian terms, the devil is the prince of the world, and the lord of progress and consequence: he is the power behind all " historical power," and so will it remain, however ill it may sound to-day in ears that are accustomed to canonise such power and consequence. The world has become skilled at giving new names to things and even baptizing the devil. It is truly an hour of great danger. Men seem to be near the discovery that the egoism of individuals, groups or masses has been at all times the lever of the " historical movements ": and yet they are in no way disturbed by the discovery, but proclaim that " egoism shall be our god." With this new faith in their hearts, they begin quite intentionally to build future history on egoism : though it must be a clever egoism, one that allows of some limitation, that it may stand firmer; one that studies history for the purpose of recognising the foolish kind of egoism. Their study has taught them that the state has a special mission in all future egoistic systems: it will be the patron of all the clever egoisms, to protect them with all the power of its military and police against the dangerous outbreaks of the other kind. There is the same idea in introducing history—natural as well as human history— among the labouring classes, whose folly makes them dangerous. For men know well that a grain of historical culture is able to break down the rough, blind instincts and desires, or to turn them to the service of a clever egoism. In fact they are beginning to think, with Edward von Hartmann, of " fixing themselves with an eye to the future in their earthly home, and making themselves comfortable there." Hartmann calls this life the " man-

hood of humanity" with an ironical reference to
what is now called "manhood";—as if only our
sober models of selfishness were embraced by it;
just as he prophesies an age of graybeards following
on this stage,—obviously another ironical glance at
our ancient time-servers. For he speaks of the ripe
discretion with which "they view all the stormy
passions of their past life and understand the vanity
of the ends they seem to have striven for." No, a
manhood of crafty and historically cultured egoism
corresponds to an old age that hangs to life with
no dignity but a horrible tenacity, where the

> "last scene of all
> That ends this strange eventful history,
> Is second childishness and mere oblivion,
> Sans teeth, sans eyes, sans taste, sans everything."

Whether the dangers of our life and culture come
from these dreary, toothless old men, or from the
so-called "men" of Hartmann, we have the right
to defend our youth with tooth and claw against
both of them, and never tire of saving the future
from these false prophets. But in this battle we
shall discover an unpleasant truth—that men intentionally help, and encourage, and use, the worst
aberrations of the historical sense from which the
present time suffers.

They use it, however, against youth, in order to
transform it into that ripe "egoism of manhood"
they so long for: they use it to overcome the natural
reluctance of the young by its magical splendour,
which unmans while it enlightens them. Yes, we
know only too well the kind of ascendency history

can gain; how it can uproot the strongest instincts
of youth, passion, courage, unselfishness and love;
can cool its feeling for justice, can crush or repress
its desire for a slow ripening by the contrary desire
to be soon productive, ready and useful; and cast
a sick doubt over all honesty and downrightness
of feeling.   It can even cozen youth of its fairest
privilege, the power of planting a great thought
with the fullest confidence, and letting it grow of
itself to a still greater thought.   An excess of
history can do all that, as we have seen, by no
longer allowing a man to feel and act *unhistorically*:
for history is continually shifting his horizon and
removing the atmosphere surrounding him.   From
an infinite horizon he withdraws into himself, back
into the small egoistic circle, where he must become
dry and withered: he may possibly attain to cleverness, but never to wisdom.   He lets himself be
talked over, is always calculating and parleying
with facts.   He is never enthusiastic, but blinks
his eyes, and understands how to look for his own
profit or his party's in the profit or loss of somebody else.   He unlearns all his useless modesty,
and turns little by little into the "man" or the
"graybeard" of Hartmann.   And that is what
they *want* him to be: that is the meaning of the
present cynical demand for the "full surrender of
the personality to the world-process"—for the
sake of his end, the redemption of the world, as
the rogue E. von Hartmann tells us.   Though
redemption can scarcely be the conscious aim
of these people: the world were better redeemed
by being redeemed from these "men" and

"graybeards."   For then would come the reign
of youth.

X.

And in this kingdom of youth I can cry Land !
Land ! Enough, and more than enough, of the
wild voyage over dark strange seas, of eternal
search and eternal disappointment ! The coast is
at last in sight. Whatever it be, we must land
there, and the worst haven is better than tossing
again in the hopeless waves of an infinite scepticism.
Let us hold fast by the land : we shall find the
good harbours later and make the voyage easier
for those who come after us.

The voyage was dangerous and exciting. How
far are we even now from that quiet state of
contemplation with which we first saw our ship
launched ! In tracking out the dangers of history,
we have found ourselves especially exposed to them.
We carry on us the marks of that sorrow which an
excess of history brings in its train to the men of
the modern time. And this present treatise, as I
will not attempt to deny, shows the modern note
of a weak personality in the intemperateness of its
criticism, the unripeness of its humanity, in the too
frequent transitions from irony to cynicism, from
arrogance to scepticism. And yet I trust in the
inspiring power that directs my vessel instead of
genius; I trust in *youth*, that has brought me on
the right road in forcing from me a protest against
the modern historical education, and a demand that
the man must learn to live, above all, and only

use history in the service of the life that he has
learned to live. He must be young to understand
this protest; and considering the premature grayness of our present youth, he can scarcely be young
enough if he would understand its reason as well.
An example will help me. In Germany, not more
than a century ago, a natural instinct for what is
called " poetry " was awakened in some young men.
Are we to think that the generations who had lived
before that time had not spoken of the art, however
really strange and unnatural it may have been
to them? We know the contrary; that they had
thought, written, and quarrelled about it with all
their might—in " words, words, words." Giving
life to such words did not prove the death of the
word-makers; in a certain sense they are living
still. For if, as Gibbon says, nothing but time—
though a long time—is needed for a world to
perish, so nothing but time—though still more
time—is needed for a false idea to be destroyed in
Germany, the " Land of Little-by-little." In any
event, there are perhaps a hundred men more now
than there were a century ago who know what
poetry is: perhaps in another century there will be
a hundred more who have learned in the meantime
what culture is, and that the Germans have had
as yet no culture, however proudly they may talk
about it. The general satisfaction of the Germans
at their culture will seem as foolish and incredible
to such men as the once lauded classicism of
Gottsched, or the reputation of Ramler as the
German Pindar, seemed to us. They will perhaps
think this " culture " to be merely a kind of know-

ledge about culture, and a false and superficial knowledge at that. False and superficial, because the Germans endured the contradiction between life and knowledge, and did not see what was characteristic in the culture of really educated peoples, that it can only rise and bloom from life. But by the Germans it is worn like a paper flower, or spread over like the icing on a cake; and so must remain a useless lie for ever.

The education of youth in Germany starts from this false and unfruitful idea of culture. Its aim, when faced squarely, is not to form the liberally educated man, but the professor, the man of science, who wants to be able to make use of his science as soon as possible, and stands on one side in order to see life clearly. The result, even from a ruthlessly practical point of view, is the historically and æsthetically trained Philistine, the babbler of old saws and new wisdom on Church, State and Art, the sensorium that receives a thousand impressions, the insatiable belly that yet knows not what true hunger and thirst is. An education with such an aim and result is against nature. But only he who is not quite drowned in it can feel that; only youth can feel it, because it still has the instinct of nature, that is the first to be broken by that education. But he who will break through that education in his turn, must come to the help of youth when called upon; must let the clear light of understanding shine on its unconscious striving, and bring it to a full, vocal consciousness. How is he to attain such a strange end?

Principally by destroying the superstition that

this kind of education is *necessary*. People think
nothing but this troublesome reality of ours is
possible.   Look through the literature of higher
education in school and college for the last ten
years, and you will be astonished—and pained—
to find how much alike all the proposals of reform
have been ; in spite of all the hesitations and violent
controversies surrounding them.   You will see how
blindly they have all adopted the old idea of the
"educated man" (in our sense) being the necessary
and reasonable basis of the system.   The mono-
tonous canon runs thus : the young man must
begin with a knowledge of culture, not even with a
knowledge of life, still less with life and the living
of it.   This knowledge of culture is forced into the
young mind in the form of historical knowledge ;
which means that his head is filled with an enormous
mass of ideas, taken second-hand from past times
and peoples, not from immediate contact with life.
He desires to experience something for himself, and
feel a close-knit, living system of experiences growing within himself.   But his desire is drowned and
dizzied in the sea of shams, as if it were possible to
sum up in a few years the highest and notablest
experiences of ancient times, and the greatest times
too.   It is the same mad method that carries our
young artists off to picture-galleries, instead of the
studio of a master, and above all the one studio
of the only master, Nature.   As if one could discover by a hasty rush through history the ideas and
technique of past times, and their individual outlook
on life !   For life itself is a kind of handicraft that
must be learned thoroughly and industriously, and

diligently practised, if we are not to have mere botchers and babblers as the issue of it all!

Plato thought it necessary for the first generation of his new society (in the perfect state) to be brought up with the help of a "mighty lie." The children were to be taught to believe that they had all lain dreaming for a long time under the earth, where they had been moulded and formed by the master-hand of Nature. It was impossible to go against the past, and work against the work of gods! And so it had to be an unbreakable law of nature, that he who is born to be a philosopher has gold in his body, the fighter has only silver, and the workman iron and bronze. As it is not possible to blend these metals, according to Plato, so there could never be any confusion between the classes: the belief in the *æterna veritas* of this arrangement was the basis of the new education and the new state. So the modern German believes also in the *æterna veritas* of his education, of his kind of culture: and yet this belief will fail—as the Platonic state would have failed—if the mighty German lie be ever opposed by the truth, that the German has no culture because he cannot build one on the basis of his education. He wishes for the flower without the root or the stalk; and so he wishes in vain. That is the simple truth, a rude and unpleasant truth, but yet a mighty one.

But our first generation must be brought up in this "mighty truth," and must suffer from it too; for it must educate itself through it, even against its own nature, to attain a new nature and manner of life, which shall yet proceed from the old. So

it might say to itself, in the old Spanish phrase,
" Defienda me Dios de my," God keep me from
myself, from the character, that is, which has been
put into me. It must taste that truth drop by drop,
like a bitter, powerful medicine. And every man
in this generation must subdue himself to pass the
judgment on his own nature, which he might pass
more easily on his whole time :—" We are without
instruction, nay, we are too corrupt to live, to see
and hear truly and simply, to understand what is
near and natural to us. We have not yet laid even
the foundations of culture, for we are not ourselves
convinced that we have a sincere life in us." We
crumble and fall asunder, our whole being is divided,
half mechanically, into an inner and outer side ;
we are sown with ideas as with dragon's teeth, and
bring forth a new dragon-brood of them ; we suffer
from the malady of words, and have no trust in any
feeling that is not stamped with its special word.
And being such a dead fabric of words and ideas,
that yet has an uncanny movement in it, I have
still perhaps the right to say *cogito ergo sum*,
though not *vivo ergo cogito*. I am permitted the
empty *esse*, not the full green *vivere*. A primary
feeling tells me that I am a thinking being but not
a living one, that I am no " animal," but at most a
" cogital." " Give me life, and I will soon make
you a culture out of it "—will be the cry of every
man in this new generation, and they will all know
each other by this cry. But who will give them
this life ?

No god and no man will give it—only their own
youth. Set this free, and you will set life free as

well. For it only lay concealed, in a prison ; it is
not yet withered or dead—ask your own selves !

But it is sick, this life that is set free, and must
be healed. It suffers from many diseases, and not
only from the memory of its chains. It suffers
from the malady which I have spoken of, the
malady of history. Excess of history has attacked
the plastic power of life, that no more understands
how to use the past as a means of strength and
nourishment. It is a fearful disease, and yet, if
youth had not a natural gift for clear vision, no
one would see that it is a disease, and that a
paradise of health has been lost. But the same
youth, with that same natural instinct of health,
has guessed how the paradise can be regained.
It knows the magic herbs and simples for the
malady of history, and the excess of it. And
what are they called ?

It is no marvel that they bear the names of
poisons :—the antidotes to history are the " unhistorical " and the " super-historical." With these
names we return to the beginning of our inquiry
and draw near to its final close.

By the word " unhistorical " I mean the power,
the art of *forgetting*, and of drawing a limited
horizon round one's self. I call the power " super-
historical " which turns the eyes from the process
of becoming to that which gives existence an
eternal and stable character, to art and religion.
Science—for it is science that makes us speak of
" poisons "—sees in these powers contrary powers :
for it considers only that view of things to be true
and right, and therefore scientific, which regards

something as finished and historical, not as continuing and eternal. Thus it lives in a deep antagonism towards the powers that make for eternity—art and religion,—for it hates the forgetfulness that is the death of knowledge, and tries to remove all limitation of horizon and cast men into an infinite boundless sea, whose waves are bright with the clear knowledge—of becoming!

If they could only live therein! Just as towns are shaken by an avalanche and become desolate, and man builds his house there in fear and for a season only; so life is broken in sunder and becomes weak and spiritless, if the avalanche of ideas started by science take from man the foundation of his rest and security, the belief in what is stable and eternal. Must life dominate knowledge, or knowledge life? Which of the two is the higher, and decisive power? There is no room for doubt: life is the higher, and the dominating power, for the knowledge that annihilated life would be itself annihilated too. Knowledge presupposes life, and has the same interest in maintaining it that every creature has in its own preservation. Science needs very careful watching: there is a hygiene of life near the volumes of science, and one of its sentences runs thus:—The unhistorical and the super-historical are the natural antidotes against the overpowering of life by history; they are the cures for the historical disease. We who are sick of the disease may suffer a little from the antidote. But this is no proof that the treatment we have chosen is wrong.

And here I see the mission of the youth that

forms the first generation of fighters and dragon-slayers: it will bring a more beautiful and blessed humanity and culture, but will have itself no more than a glimpse of the promised land of happiness and wondrous beauty. This youth will suffer both from the malady and its antidotes: and yet it believes in strength and health and boasts a nature closer to the great Nature than its forebears, the cultured men and graybeards of the present. But its mission is to shake to their foundations the present conceptions of "health" and "culture," and erect hatred and scorn in the place of this rococo mass of ideas. And the clearest sign of its own strength and health is just the fact that it can use no idea, no party-cry from the present-day mint of words and ideas to symbolise its own existence: but only claims conviction from the power in it that acts and fights, breaks up and destroys; and from an ever heightened feeling of life when the hour strikes. You may deny this youth any culture—but how would youth count that a reproach? You may speak of its rawness and intemperateness—but it is not yet old and wise enough to be acquiescent. It need not pretend to a ready-made culture at all; but enjoys all the rights—and the consolations—of youth, especially the right of brave unthinking honesty and the consolation of an inspiring hope.

I know that such hopeful beings understand all these truisms from within, and can translate them into a doctrine for their own use, through their personal experience. To the others there will appear, in the meantime, nothing but a row of covered dishes, that may perhaps seem empty: until they see one day with astonished eyes that the dishes are full, and that all ideas and impulses and passions are massed together in these truisms that cannot lie covered for long. I leave those doubting ones to time, that brings all things to light; and turn at last to that great company of hope, to tell them the way and the course of their salvation, their rescue from the disease of history, and their own history as well, in a parable; whereby they may again become healthy enough to study history anew, and under the guidance of life make use of the past in that threefold way—monumental, antiquarian, or critical. At first they will be more ignorant than the " educated men " of the present: for they will have unlearnt much and have lost any desire even to discover what those educated men especially wish to know: in fact, their chief mark from the educated point of view will be just their want of science; their indifference and inaccessibility to all the good and famous things. But at the end of the cure, they are men again and have ceased to be mere shadows of humanity. That is something; there is yet hope, and do not ye who hope laugh in your hearts?

How can we reach that end? you will ask. The Delphian god cries his oracle to you at the beginning of your wanderings, " Know thyself." It is a hard saying: for that god " tells nothing and conceals nothing but merely points the way," as Heraclitus said. But whither does he point?

In certain epochs the Greeks were in a similar danger of being overwhelmed by what was past and foreign, and perishing on the rock of "history." They never lived proud and untouched. Their "culture" was for a long time a chaos of foreign forms and ideas,—Semitic, Babylonian, Lydian and Egyptian,—and their religion a battle of all the gods of the East; just as German culture and religion is at present a death-struggle of all foreign nations and bygone times. And yet, Hellenic culture was no mere mechanical unity, thanks to that Delphic oracle. The Greeks gradually learned to organise the chaos, by taking Apollo's advice and thinking back to themselves, to their own true necessities, and letting all the sham necessities go. Thus they again came into possession of themselves, and did not remain long the Epigoni of the whole East, burdened with their inheritance. After that hard fight, they increased and enriched the treasure they had inherited by their obedience to the oracle, and they became the ancestors and models for all the cultured nations of the future.

This is a parable for each one of us: he must organise the chaos in himself by "thinking himself back" to his true needs. He will want all his honesty, all the sturdiness and sincerity in his character to help him to revolt against second-hand thought, second-hand learning, second-hand action. And he will begin then to understand that culture can be something more than a "decoration of life"—a concealment and disfiguring of it, in other words; for all adornment hides what is adorned. And thus the Greek idea, as against the Roman, will be discovered to him, the idea of culture as a new and finer nature, without distinction of inner and outer, without convention or disguise, as a unity of thought and will, life and appearance. He will learn too, from his own experience, that it was by a greater force of moral character that the Greeks were victorious, and that everything which makes for sincerity is a further step towards true culture, however this sincerity may harm the ideals of education that are reverenced at the time, or even have power to shatter a whole system of merely decorative culture.

SCHOPENHAUER AS
EDUCATOR.

SCHOPENHAUER AS EDUCATOR.

I.

When the traveller, who had seen many countries and nations and continents, was asked what common attribute he had found everywhere existing among men, he answered, " They have a tendency to sloth." Many may think that the fuller truth would have been, " They are all timid." They hide themselves behind " manners " and " opinions." At bottom every man knows well enough that he is a unique being, only once on this earth ; and by no extra-ordinary chance will such a marvellously picturesque piece of diversity in unity as he is, ever be put to-gether a second time. He knows this, but hides it like an evil conscience ;—and why ? From fear of his neighbour, who looks for the latest conven-tionalities in him, and is wrapped up in them himself. But what is it that forces the man to fear his neighbour, to think and act with his herd, and not seek his own joy ? Shyness perhaps, in a few rare cases, but in the majority it is idleness,

the " taking things easily," in a word the " tendency
to sloth," of which the traveller spoke. He was
right; men are more slothful than timid, and their
greatest fear is of the burdens that an uncom-
promising honesty and nakedness of speech and
action would lay on them. It is only the artists
who hate this lazy wandering in borrowed manners
and ill-fitting opinions, and discover the secret of
the evil conscience, the truth that each human
being is a unique marvel. They show us, how in
every little movement of his muscles the man is
an individual self, and further—as an analytical
deduction from his individuality—a beautiful and
interesting object, a new and incredible phenomenon
(as is every work of nature), that can never become
tedious. If the great thinker despise mankind, it
is for their laziness; they seem mere indifferent
bits of pottery, not worth any commerce or im-
provement. The man who will not belong to the
general mass, has only to stop " taking himself
easily"; to follow his conscience, which cries out
to him, " Be thyself! all that thou doest and
thinkest and desirest, is not—thyself!"

Every youthful soul hears this cry day and night,
and quivers to hear it: for she divines the sum
of happiness that has been from eternity destined
for her, if she think of her true deliverance; and
towards this happiness she can in no wise be
helped, so long as she lies in the chains of Opinion
and of Fear. And how comfortless and unmeaning
may life become without this deliverance! There
is no more desolate or Ishmaelitish creature in nature
than the man who has broken away from his true

genius, and does nothing but peer aimlessly about him.   There is no reason to attack such a man at all, for he is a mere husk without a kernel, a painted cloth, tattered and sagging, a scarecrow ghost, that can rouse no fear, and certainly no pity. And though one be right in saying of a sluggard that he is "killing time," yet in respect of an age that rests its salvation on public opinion,—that is, on private laziness,—one must be quite determined that such a time shall be " killed," once and for all : I mean that it shall be blotted from life's true History of Liberty.   Later generations will be greatly disgusted, when they come to treat the movements of a period in which no living men ruled, but shadow-men on the screen of public opinion ; and to some far posterity our age may well be the darkest chapter of history, the most unknown because the least human.   I have walked through the new streets of our cities, and thought how of all the dreadful houses that these gentlemen with their public opinion have built for themselves, not a stone will remain in a hundred years, and that the opinions of these busy masons may well have fallen with them.   But how full of hope should they all be who feel that they are no citizens of this age !   If they were, they would have to help on the work of " killing their time," and of perishing with it,—when they wish rather to quicken the time to life, and in that life themselves to *live*.

But even if the future leave us nothing to hope for, the wonderful fact of our existing at this present moment of time gives us the greatest encouragement to live after our own rule and measure ;

so inexplicable is it, that we should be living just
to-day, though there have been an infinity of time
wherein we might have arisen; that we own
nothing but a span's length of it, this "to-day,"
and must show in it wherefore and whereunto we
have arisen. We have to answer for our existence
to ourselves; and will therefore be our own true
pilots, and not admit that our being resembles a
blind fortuity. One must take a rather impudent
and reckless way with the riddle; especially as the
key is apt to be lost, however things turn out. Why
cling to your bit of earth, or your little business,
or listen to what your neighbour says? It is so
provincial to bind oneself to views which are no
longer binding a couple of hundred miles away.
East and West are signs that somebody chalks up
in front of us to fool such cowards as we are. "I
will make the attempt to gain freedom," says the
youthful soul; and will be hindered, just because
two nations happen to hate each other and go to
war, or because there is a sea between two parts
of the earth, or a religion is taught in the vicinity,
which did not exist two thousand years ago. "And
this is not—thyself," the soul says. "No one can
build thee the bridge, over which thou must cross
the river of life, save thyself alone. There are paths
and bridges and demi-gods without number, that
will gladly carry thee over, but only at the price
of thine own self: thy self wouldst thou have to
give in pawn, and then lose it. There is in the
world one road whereon none may go, except thou:
ask not whither it lead, but go forward. Who was
it that spake that true word—'A man has never

risen higher than when he knoweth not whither his
road may yet lead him'?"

But how can we "find ourselves" again, and how
can man "know himself"?   He is a thing obscure
and veiled : if the hare have seven skins, man can
cast from him seventy times seven, and yet will
not be able to say "Here art thou in very truth ;
this is outer shell no more."   Also this digging
into one's self, this straight, violent descent into the
pit of one's being, is a troublesome and dangerous
business to start.   A man may easily take such
hurt, that no physician can heal him.   And again,
what were the use, since everything bears witness
to our essence,—our friendships and enmities, our
looks and greetings, our memories and forgetful-
nesses, our books and our writing!   This is the
most effective way :—to let the youthful soul look
back on life with the question, "What hast thou
up to now truly loved, what has drawn thy soul
upward, mastered it and blessed it too?"   Set up
these things that thou hast honoured before thee,
and, maybe, they will show thee, in their being
and their order, a law which is the fundamental
law of thine own self.   Compare these objects,
consider how one completes and broadens and
transcends and explains another, how they form
a ladder on which thou hast all the time been
climbing to thy self: for thy true being lies not
deeply hidden in thee, but an infinite height above
thee, or at least above that which thou dost
commonly take to be thyself.   The true educators
and moulders reveal to thee the real groundwork
and import of thy being, something that in itself

cannot be moulded or educated, but is anyhow difficult of approach, bound and crippled: thy educators can be nothing but thy deliverers. And that is the secret of all culture: it does not give artificial limbs, wax noses, or spectacles for the eyes—a thing that could buy such gifts is but the base coin of education. But it is rather a liberation, a removal of all the weeds and rubbish and vermin that attack the delicate shoots, the streaming forth of light and warmth, the tender dropping of the night rain; it is the following and the adoring of Nature when she is pitifully-minded as a mother;—her completion, when it bends before her fierce and ruthless blasts and turns them to good, and draws a veil over all expression of her tragic unreason—for she is a step-mother too, sometimes.

There are other means of "finding ourselves," of coming to ourselves out of the confusion wherein we all wander as in a dreary cloud; but I know none better than to think on our educators. So I will to-day take as my theme the hard teacher Arthur Schopenhauer, and speak of others later.

II.

In order to describe properly what an event my first look into Schopenhauer's writings was for me, I must dwell for a minute on an idea, that recurred more constantly in my youth, and touched me more nearly, than any other. I wandered then as I pleased in a world of wishes, and thought that

destiny would relieve me of the dreadful and
wearisome duty of educating myself: some philosopher would come at the right moment to do it
for me,—some true philosopher, who could be
obeyed without further question, as he would be
trusted more than one's self. Then I said within
me : " What would be the principles, on which he
might teach thee ? "   And I pondered in my mind
what he would say to the two maxims of education
that hold the field in our time. The first demands
that the teacher should find out at once the strong
point in his pupil, and then direct all his skill and
will, all the moisture and all the sunshine, to bring
the fruit of that single virtue to maturity. The
second requires him to raise to a higher power all
the qualities that already exist, cherish them and
bring them into a harmonious relation. But, we
may ask, should one who has a decided talent for
working in gold be made for that reason to learn
music ?   And can we admit that Benvenuto
Cellini's father was right in continually forcing
him back to the "dear little horn"—the "cursed
piping," as his son called it ? We cannot think so
in the case of such a strong and clearly marked
talent as his, and it may well be that this maxim
of harmonious development applies only to weaker
natures, in which there is a whole swarm of desires
and inclinations, though they may not amount to
very much, singly or together. On the other hand,
where do we find such a blending of harmonious voices—nay, the soul of harmony itself—as we
see in natures like Cellini's, where everything—
knowledge, desire, love and hate—tends towards a

single point, the root of all, and a harmonious
system, the resultant of the various forces, is built
up through the irresistible domination of this vital
centre? And so perhaps the two maxims are not
contrary at all : the one merely saying that man
must have a centre, the other, a circumference as
well. The philosophic teacher of my dream would
not only discover the central force, but would know
how to prevent its being destructive of the other
powers : his task, I thought, would be the welding
of the whole man into a solar system with life and
movement, and the discovery of its paraphysical
laws.

In the meantime I could not find my philosopher,
however I tried ; I saw how badly we moderns
compare with the Greeks and Romans, even in the
serious study of educational problems. You can
go through all Germany, and especially all the
universities, with this need in your heart, and will
not find what you seek ; many humbler wishes
than that are still unfulfilled there. For example,
if a German seriously wish to make himself an
orator, or to enter a "school for authors," he will
find neither master nor school : no one yet seems
to have thought that speaking and writing are arts
which cannot be learnt without the most careful
method and untiring application. But, to their
shame, nothing shows more clearly the insolent
self-satisfaction of our people than the lack of
demand for educators; it comes partly from meanness, partly from want of thought. Anything will
do as a so-called "family tutor," even among our
most eminent and cultured people : and what a

menagerie of crazy heads and mouldy devices mostly go to make up the belauded Gymnasium! And consider what we are satisfied with in our finishing schools,—our universities. Look at our professors and their institutions! And compare the difficulty of the task of educating a man to be a man! Above all, the wonderful way in which the German savants fall to their dish of knowledge, shows that they are thinking more of Science than mankind; and they are trained to lead a forlorn hope in her service, in order to encourage ever new generations to the same sacrifice. If their traffic with knowledge be not limited and controlled by any more general principles of education, but allowed to run on indefinitely,—"the more the better,"—it is as harmful to learning as the economic theory of *laisser faire* to common morality. No one recognises now that the education of the professors is an exceedingly difficult problem, if their humanity is not to be sacrificed or shrivelled up:—this difficulty can be actually seen in countless examples of natures warped and twisted by their reckless and premature devotion to science. There is a still more important testimony to the complete absence of higher education, pointing to a greater and more universal danger. It is clear at once why an orator or writer cannot now be educated,—because there are no teachers; and why a savant must be a distorted and perverted thing,—because he will have been trained by the inhuman abstraction, science. This being so, let a man ask himself: "Where are now the types of moral excellence and fame for all our generation—

learned and unlearned, high and low—the visible
abstract of constructive ethics for this age ?   Where
has vanished all the reflection on moral questions
that has occupied every great developed society at
all epochs ? "   There is no fame for that now, and
there are none to reflect : we are really drawing on
the inherited moral capital which our predecessors
accumulated for us, and which we do not know
how to increase, but only to squander.   Such things
are either not mentioned in our society, or, if at all,
with a naïve want of personal experience that
makes one disgusted.   It comes to this, that our
schools and professors simply turn aside from any
moral instruction or content themselves with
formulæ ; virtue is a word and nothing more, on
both sides, an old-fashioned word that they laugh
at—and it is worse when they do not laugh, for
then they are hypocrites.

An explanation of this faint-heartedness and
ebbing of all moral strength would be difficult and
complex: but whoever is considering the influence
of Christianity in its hour of victory on the
morality of the mediæval world, must not forget
that it reacts also in its defeat, which is apparently
its position to-day.   By its lofty ideal, Christianity
has outbidden the ancient Systems of Ethics and
their invariable naturalism, with which men came
to feel a dull disgust: and afterwards when they
did reach the knowledge of what was better and
higher, they found they had no longer the power,
for all their desire, to return to its embodiment in
the antique virtues.   And so the life of the modern
man is passed in see-sawing between Christianity

and Paganism, between a furtive or hypocritical approach to Christian morality, and an equally shy and spiritless dallying with the antique: and he does not thrive under it. His inherited fear of naturalism, and its more recent attraction for him, his desire to come to rest somewhere, while in the impotence of his intellect he swings backwards and forwards between the "good" and the "better" course—all this argues an instability in the modern mind that condemns it to be without joy or fruit. Never were moral teachers more necessary and never were they more unlikely to be found: physicians are most in danger themselves in times when they are most needed and many men are sick. For where are our modern physicians who are strong and sure-footed enough to hold up another or lead him by the hand? There lies a certain heavy gloom on the best men of our time, an eternal loathing for the battle that is fought in their hearts between honesty and lies, a wavering of trust in themselves, which makes them quite incapable of showing to others the way they must go.

So I was right in speaking of my "wandering in a world of wishes" when I dreamt of finding a true philosopher who could lift me from the slough of insufficiency, and teach me again simply and honestly to be in my thoughts and life, in the deepest sense of the word, "out of season"; simply and honestly—for men have now become such complicated machines that they must be dishonest, if they speak at all, or wish to act on their words.

With such needs and desires within me did I come to know Schopenhauer.

VOL. II.   H

I belong to those readers of Schopenhauer who know perfectly well, after they have turned the first page, that they will read all the others, and listen to every word that he has spoken. My trust in him sprang to life at once, and has been the same for nine years. I understood him as though he had written for me (this is the most intelligible, though a rather foolish and conceited way of expressing it). Hence I never found a paradox in him, though occasionally some small errors: for paradoxes are only assertions that carry no conviction, because the author has made them himself without any conviction, wishing to appear brilliant, or to mislead, or, above all, to pose. Schopenhauer never poses: he writes for himself, and no one likes to be deceived—least of all a philosopher who has set this up as his law: " deceive nobody, not even thyself," neither with the " white lies " of all social intercourse, which writers almost unconsciously imitate, still less with the more conscious deceits of the platform, and the artificial methods of rhetoric. Schopenhauer's speeches are to himself alone; or if you like to imagine an auditor, let it be a son whom the father is instructing. It is a rough, honest, good-humoured talk to one who " hears and loves." Such writers are rare. His strength and sanity surround us at the first sound of his voice: it is like entering the heights of the forest, where we breathe deep and are well again. We feel a bracing air everywhere, a certain candour and naturalness of his own, that belongs to men who are at home with themselves, and masters of a

very rich home indeed: he is quite different from
the writers who are surprised at themselves if they
have said something intelligent, and whose pronouncements for that reason have something
nervous and unnatural about them. We are just
as little reminded in Schopenhauer of the professor with his stiff joints worse for want of
exercise, his narrow chest and scraggy figure, his
slinking or strutting gait. And again his rough
and rather grim soul leads us not so much to
miss as to despise the suppleness and courtly
grace of the excellent Frenchmen; and no one
will find in him the gilded imitations of pseudo-
gallicism that our German writers prize so highly.
His style in places reminds me a little of Goethe,
but is not otherwise on any German model. For
he knows how to be profound with simplicity,
striking without rhetoric, and severely logical
without pedantry: and of what German could he
have learnt that? He also keeps free from the
hair-splitting, jerky and (with all respect) rather
un-German manner of Lessing: no small merit
in him, for Lessing is the most tempting of all
models for prose style. The highest praise I can
give his manner of presentation is to apply his
own phrase to himself:—" A philosopher must be
very honest to avail himself of no aid from poetry
or rhetoric."   That honesty is something, and even
a virtue, is one of those private opinions which are
forbidden in this age of public opinion; and so I
shall not be praising Schopenhauer, but only giving
him a distinguishing mark, when I repeat that he
is honest, even as a writer: so few of them are

that we are apt to mistrust every one who writes
at all. I only know a single author that I can
rank with Schopenhauer, or even above him, in
the matter of honesty; and that is Montaigne.
The joy of living on this earth is increased by the
existence of such a man. The effect on myself,
at any rate, since my first acquaintance with that
strong and masterful spirit, has been, that I can
say of him as he of Plutarch—"As soon as I open
him, I seem to grow a pair of wings." If I had
the task of making myself at home on the earth,
I would choose him as my companion.

Schopenhauer has a second characteristic in
common with Montaigne, besides honesty; a joy
that really makes others joyful. "Aliis lætus,
sibi sapiens." There are two very different kinds
of joyfulness. The true thinker always communi-
cates joy and life, whether he is showing his serious
or comic side, his human insight or his godlike
forbearance: without surly looks or trembling
hands or watery eyes, but simply and truly, with
fearlessness and strength, a little cavalierly perhaps,
and sternly, but always as a conqueror: and it is
this that brings the deepest and intensest joy, to
see the conquering god with all the monsters that
he has fought. But the joyfulness one finds here
and there in the mediocre writers and limited
thinkers makes some of us miserable; I felt this,
for example, with the "joyfulness" of David Strauss.
We are generally ashamed of such a quality in our
contemporaries, because they show the nakedness
of our time, and of the men in it, to posterity.
Such *fils de joie* do not see the sufferings and

the monsters, that they pretend, as philosophers, to see and fight; and so their joy deceives us, and we hate it; it tempts to the false belief that they have gained some victory. At bottom there is only joy where there is victory: and this applies to true philosophy as much as to any work of art. The contents may be forbidding and serious, as the problem of existence always is; the work will only prove tiresome and oppressive, if the slipshod thinker and the dilettante have spread the mist of their insufficiency over it: while nothing happier or better can come to man's lot than to be near one of those conquering spirits whose profound thought has made them love what is most vital, and whose wisdom has found its goal in beauty. They really speak: they are no stammerers or babblers; they live and move, and have no part in the *danse macabre* of the rest of humanity. And so in their company one feels a natural man again, and could cry out with Goethe—"What a wondrous and priceless thing is a living creature! How fitted to his surroundings, how true, and real!"

I have been describing nothing but the first, almost physiological, impression made upon me by Schopenhauer, the magical emanation of inner force from one plant of Nature to another, that follows the slightest contact. Analysing it, I find that this influence of Schopenhauer has three elements, his honesty, his joy, and his consistency. He is honest, as speaking and writing for himself alone; joyful, because his thought has conquered the greatest difficulties; consistent, because he cannot help being so. His strength rises like a flame in the calm air, straight up, without a tremor or deviation. He finds his way, without our noticing that he has been seeking it: so surely and cleverly and inevitably does he run his course, as if by some law of gravitation. If any one have felt what it means to find, in our present world of Centaurs and Chimæras, a single-hearted and unaffected child of nature who moves unconstrained on his own road, he will understand my joy and surprise in discovering Schopenhauer: I knew in him the educator and philosopher I had so long desired. Only, however, in his writings: which was a great loss. All the more did I exert myself to see behind the book the living man whose testament it was, and who promised his inheritance to such as could, and would, be more than his readers—his pupils and his sons.

III.

I get profit from a philosopher, just so far as he can be an example to me. There is no doubt that a man can draw whole nations after him by his example; as is shown by Indian history, which is practically the history of Indian philosophy. But this example must exist in his outward life, not merely in his books; it must follow the way of the Grecian philosophers, whose doctrine was in their dress and bearing and general manner of life rather than in their speech or writing. We have nothing yet of this " breathing testimony " in German philo-

sophical life; the spirit has, apparently, long completed its emancipation, while the flesh has hardly
begun ; yet it is foolish to think that the spirit can
be really free and independent when this victory
over limitation—which is ultimately a formative
limiting of one's self—is not embodied anew in
every look and movement. Kant held to his
university, submitted to its regulations, and be-
longed, as his colleagues and students thought, to
a definite religious faith : and naturally his example
has produced, above all, University professors of
philosophy. Schopenhauer makes small account
of the learned tribe, keeps himself exclusive, and
cultivates an independence from state and society
as his ideal, to escape the chains of circumstance
here : that is his value to us. Many steps in the
enfranchisement of the philosopher are unknown
in Germany; they cannot always remain so. Our
artists live more bravely and honourably than our
philosophers ; and Richard Wagner, the best
example of all, shows how genius need not fear a
fight to the death with the established forms and
ordinances, if we wish to bring the higher truth
and order, that lives in him, to the light. The
"truth," however, of which we hear so much from
our professors, seems to be a far more modest
being, and no kind of disturbance is to be feared
from her; she is an easy-going and pleasant
creature, who is continually assuring the powers
that be that no one need fear any trouble from
her quarter : for man is only "pure reason." And
therefore I will say, that philosophy in Germany
has more and more to learn not to be "pure

reason": and it may well take as its model
" Schopenhauer the man."

It is no less than a marvel that he should have
come to be this human kind of example: for he
was beset, within and without, by the most frightful
dangers, that would have crushed and broken a
weaker nature.   I think there was a strong likeli-
hood of Schopenhauer the man going under, and
leaving at best a residue of " pure reason": and
only " at best"—it was more probable that neither
man nor reason would survive.

A modern Englishman sketches the most usual
danger to extraordinary men who live in a society
that worships the ordinary, in this manner:—" Such
uncommon characters are first cowed, then become
sick and melancholy, and then die. A Shelley
could never have lived in England: a race of
Shelleys would have been impossible." Our
Hölderins and Kleists were undone by their un-
conventionality, and were not strong enough for
the climate of the so-called German culture; and
only iron natures like Beethoven, Goethe, Schopenhauer and Wagner could hold out against it.   Even
in them the effect of this weary toiling and moil-
ing is seen in many lines and wrinkles; their
breathing is harder and their voice is forced.   The
old diplomatist who had only just seen and spoken
to Goethe, said to a friend—" Voilà un homme qui
a eu de grands chagrins ! " which Goethe translated
to mean " That is a man who has taken great pains
in his life."   And he adds, " If the trace of the
sorrow and activity we have gone through cannot
be wiped from our features, it is no wonder that

all that survives of us and our struggles should
bear the same impress." And this is the Goethe
to whom our cultured Philistines point as the
happiest of Germans, that they may prove their
thesis, that it must be possible to be happy among
them—with the unexpressed corollary that no one
can be pardoned for feeling unhappy and lonely
among them. Hence they push their doctrine, in
practice, to its merciless conclusion, that there is
always a secret guilt in isolation. Poor Schopenhauer had this secret guilt too in his heart, the
guilt of cherishing his philosophy more than his
fellow-men; and he was so unhappy as to have
learnt from Goethe that he must defend his philosophy at all costs from the neglect of his contemporaries, to save its very existence: for there is a
kind of Grand Inquisitor's Censure in which the
Germans, according to Goethe, are great adepts:
it is called—inviolable silence. This much at least
was accomplished by it;—the greater part of the
first edition of Schopenhauer's masterpiece had to
be turned into waste paper. The imminent risk that
his great work would be undone, merely by neglect,
bred in him a state of unrest—perilous and uncon-
trollable;—for no single adherent of any note
presented himself. It is tragic to watch his search
for any evidence of recognition: and his piercing
cry of triumph at last, that he would now really be
read (*legor et legar*), touches us with a thrill of
pain. All the traits in which we do not see the
great philosopher show us the suffering man,
anxious for his noblest possessions; he was tortured
by the fear of losing his little property, and perhaps

of no longer being able to maintain in its purity his truly antique attitude towards philosophy. He often chose falsely in his desire to find real trust and compassion in men, only to return with a heavy heart to his faithful dog again. He was absolutely alone, with no single friend of his own kind to comfort him ; and between one and none there lies an infinity—as ever between something and nothing. No one who has true friends knows what real loneliness means, though he may have the whole world in antagonism round him. Ah, I see well ye do not know what isolation is ! Whenever there are great societies with governments and religions and public opinions—where there is a tyranny, in short, there will the lonely philosopher be hated : for philosophy offers an asylum to mankind where no tyranny can penetrate, the inner sanctuary, the centre of the heart's labyrinth : and the tyrants are galled at it. Here do the lonely men lie hid : but here too lurks their greatest danger. These men who have saved their inner freedom, must also live and be seen in the outer world : they stand in countless human relations by their birth, position, education and country, their own circumstances and the importunity of others : and so they are presumed to hold an immense number of opinions, simply because these happen to prevail : every look that is not a denial counts as an assent, every motion of the hand that does not destroy is regarded as an aid. These free and lonely men know that they perpetually seem other than they are. While they wish for nothing but truth and honesty, they are in a net of misunderstanding; and that ardent desire cannot prevent a mist of false opinions, of adaptations and wrong conclusions, of partial misapprehension and intentional reticence, from gathering round their actions. And there settles a cloud of melancholy on their brows: for such natures hate the necessity of pretence worse than death: and the continual bitterness gives them a threatening and volcanic character. They take revenge from time to time for their forced concealment and self-restraint: they issue from their dens with lowering looks: their words and deeds are explosive, and may lead to their own destruction. Schopenhauer lived amid dangers of this sort. Such lonely men need love, and friends, to whom they can be as open and sincere as to themselves, and in whose presence the deadening silence and hypocrisy may cease. Take their friends away, and there is left an increasing peril; Heinrich von Kleist was broken by the lack of love, and the most terrible weapon against unusual men is to drive them into themselves; and then their issuing forth again is a volcanic eruption. Yet there are always some demi-gods who can bear life under these fearful conditions and can be their conquerors: and if you would hear their lonely chant, listen to the music of Beethoven.

So the first danger in whose shadow Schopenhauer lived was—isolation. The second is called —doubting of the truth. To this every thinker is liable who sets out from the philosophy of Kant, provided he be strong and sincere in his sorrows and his desires, and not a mere tinkling thought-box or calculating machine. We all know the shameful state of things implied by this last reservation, and I believe it is only a very few men that Kant has so vitally affected as to change the current of their blood. To judge from what one reads, there must have been a revolution in every domain of thought since the work of this unobtrusive professor: I cannot believe it myself. For I see men, though darkly, as themselves needing to be revolutionised, before any "domains of thought" can be so. In fact, we find the first mark of any influence Kant may have had on the popular mind, in a corrosive scepticism and relativity. But it is only in noble and active spirits who could never rest in doubt that the shattering despair of truth itself could take the place of doubt. This was, for example, the effect of the Kantian philosophy on Heinrich von Kleist. "It was only a short time ago," he writes in his poignant way, "that I became acquainted with the Kantian philosophy; and I will tell you my thought, though I cannot fear that it will rack you to your inmost soul, as it did me.—We cannot decide, whether what we call truth is really truth, or whether it only seems so to us. If the latter, the truth that we amass here does not exist after death, and all our struggle to gain a possession that may follow us even to the grave is in vain. If the blade of this thought do not cut your heart, yet laugh not at another who feels himself wounded by it in his Holy of Holies. My one highest aim has vanished, and I have no more." Yes, when will men feel again deeply as Kleist did, and learn

to measure a philosophy by what it means to the
" Holy of Holies"?   And yet we must make this
estimate of what Schopenhauer can mean to us,
after Kant, as the first pioneer to bring us from
the heights of sceptical disillusionment or " critical "
renunciation, to the greater height of tragic contemplation, the nocturnal heaven with its endless
crown of stars.   His greatness is that he can stand
opposite the picture of life, and interpret it to us
as a whole: while all the clever people cannot
escape the error of thinking one comes nearer to
the interpretation by a laborious analysis of the
colours and material of the picture; with the confession, probably, that the texture of the canvas
is very complicated, and the chemical composition
of the colours undiscoverable.   Schopenhauer knew
that one must guess the painter in order to understand the picture.   But now the whole learned
fraternity is engaged on understanding the colours
and canvas, and not the picture: and only he who
has kept the universal panorama of life and being
firmly before his eyes, will use the individual
sciences without harm to himself; for, without
this general view as a norm, they are threads that
lead nowhere and only confuse still more the maze
of our existence.   Here we see, as I said, the
greatness of Schopenhauer, that he follows up
every idea, as Hamlet follows the Ghost, without
allowing himself to turn aside for a learned
digression, or be drawn away by the scholastic
abstractions of a rabid dialectic.   The study of
the minute philosophers is only interesting for the
recognition that they have reached those stages

in the great edifice of philosophy where learned
disquisitions for and against, where hair-splitting
objections and counter-objections are the rule:
and for that reason they evade the demand of
every great philosophy to speak *sub specie
æternitatis*—"this is the picture of the whole of
life: learn thence the meaning of thine own life."
And the converse: "read thine own life, and
understand thence the hieroglyphs of the universal
life." In this way must Schopenhauer's philosophy
always be interpreted; as an individualist
philosophy, starting from the single man, in his
own nature, to gain an insight into his personal
miseries, and needs, and limitations, and find out
the remedies that will console them: namely, the
sacrifice of the ego, and its submission to the
nobler ends, especially those of justice and mercy.
He teaches us to distinguish between the true and
the apparent furtherance of man's happiness: how
neither the attainment of riches, nor honour, nor
learning, can raise the individual from his deep
despair at his unworthiness; and how the quest
for these good things can only have meaning
through a universal end that transcends and
explains them;—the gaining of power to aid our
physical nature by them and, as far as may be,
correct its folly and awkwardness. For one's self
only, in the first instance: and finally, through
one's self, for all. It is a task that leads to scepticism: for there is so much to be made better yet,
in one and all!

Applying this to Schopenhauer himself, we
come to the third and most intimate danger in

which he lived, and which lay deep in the marrow
of his being. Every one is apt to discover a
limitation in himself, in his gifts of intellect as well
as his moral will, that fills him with yearning and
melancholy; and as he strives after holiness
through a consciousness of sin, so, as an intellectual
being, he has a deep longing after the "genius"
in himself. This is the root of all true culture;
and if we say this means the aspiration of man to
be "born again" as saint and genius, I know that
one need not be a Buddhist to understand the
myth. We feel a strong loathing when we find
talent without such aspiration, in the circle of the
learned, or among the so-called educated; for we
see that such men, with all their cleverness, are no
aid but a hindrance to the beginnings of culture
and the blossoming of genius, the aim of all
culture. There is a rigidity in them, parallel to
the cold arrogance of conventional virtue, which
also remains at the opposite pole to true holiness.
Schopenhauer's nature contained an extraordinarily dangerous dualism. Few thinkers have felt
as he did the complete and unmistakable certainty
of genius within them; and his genius made him
the highest of all promises,—that there could be no
deeper furrow than that which he was ploughing
in the ground of the modern world. He knew one
half of his being to be fulfilled according to its
strength, with no other need; and he followed
with greatness and dignity his vocation of con-
solidating his victory. In the other half there was
a gnawing aspiration, which we can understand,
when we hear that he turned away with a sad look

from the picture of Rancé, the founder of the
Trappists, with the words: "That is a matter of
grace." For genius evermore yearns after holiness
as it sees further and more clearly from its watch-
tower than other men, deep into the reconciliation
of Thought and Being, the kingdom of peace and
the denial of the will, and up to that other shore,
of which the Indians speak. The wonder is, that
Schopenhauer's nature should have been so incon-
ceivably stable and unshakable that it could
neither be destroyed nor petrified by this yearning.
Every one will understand this after the measure
of his own character and greatness: none of us will
understand it in the fulness of its meaning.

The more one considers these three dangers, the
more extraordinary will appear his vigour in
opposing them and his safety after the battle.
True, he gained many scars and open wounds:
and a cast of mind that may seem somewhat too
bitter and pugnacious. But his single ideal transcends the highest humanity in him. Schopenhauer
stands as a pattern to men, in spite of all those
scars and scratches. We may even say, that what
was imperfect and "all too human" in him, brings
us nearer to him as a man, for we see a sufferer
and a kinsman to suffering, not merely a dweller
on the unattainable heights of genius.

These three constitutional dangers that threat-
ened Schopenhauer, threaten us all. Each one
of us bears a creative solitude within himself,
and his consciousness of it forms an exotic aura of
strangeness round him. Most men cannot endure
it, because they are slothful, as I said, and because

their solitude hangs round them a chain of troubles and burdens. No doubt, for the man with this heavy chain, life loses almost everything that one desires from it in youth—joy, safety, honour: his fellow-men pay him his due of—isolation! The wilderness and the cave are about him, wherever he may live. He must look to it that he be not enslaved and oppressed, and become melancholy thereby. And let him surround himself with the pictures of good and brave fighters such as Schopenhauer.

The second danger, too, is not rare. Here and there we find one dowered by nature with a keen vision; his thoughts dance gladly in the witches' Sabbath of dialectic; and if he uncautiously give his talent the rein, it is easy to lose all humanity and live a ghostly life in the realm of "pure reason": or through the constant search for the "pros and cons" of things, he may go astray from the truth and live without courage or confidence, in doubt, denial and discontent, and the slender hope that waits on disillusion: "No dog could live long thus!"

The third danger is a moral or intellectual hardening: man breaks the bond that united him to his ideal: he ceases to be fruitful and reproduce himself in this or that province, and becomes an enemy or a parasite of culture. The solitude of his being has become an indivisible, unrelated atom, an icy stone. And one can perish of this solitude as well as of the fear of it, of one's self as well as one's self-sacrifice, of both aspiration and petrifaction: and to live is ever to be in danger.

Beside these dangers to which Schopenhauer would have been constitutionally liable, in whatever century he had lived, there were also some produced by his own time; and it is essential to distinguish between these two kinds, in order to grasp the typical and formative elements in his nature. The philosopher casts his eye over existence, and wishes to give it a new standard value; for it has been the peculiar task of all great thinkers to be law-givers for the weight and stamp in the mint of reality. And his task will be hindered if the men he sees near him be a weakly and worm-eaten growth. To be correct in his calculation of existence, the unworthiness of the present time must be a very small item in the addition. The study of ancient or foreign history is valuable, if at all, for a correct judgment on the whole destiny of man; which must be drawn not only from an average estimate but from a comparison of the highest destinies that can befall individuals or nations. The present is too much with us; it directs the vision even against the philosopher's will: and it will inevitably be reckoned too high in the final sum. And so he must put a low figure on his own time as against others, and suppress the present in his picture of life, as well as in himself; must put it into the background or paint it over; a difficult, and almost impossible task. The judgment of the ancient Greek philosophers on the value of existence means so much more than our own, because they had the full bloom of life itself before them, and their vision was untroubled by any felt dualism between their wish for freedom and beauty on the grand scale, and their search after truth, with its single question " What is the real *worth* of life ? " Empedocles lived when Greek culture was full to overflowing with the joy of life, and all ages may take profit from his words; especially as no other great philosopher of that great time ventured to contradict them. Empedocles is only the clearest voice among them —they all say the same thing, if a man will but open his ears. A modern thinker is always in the throes of an unfulfilled desire; he is looking for life,—warm, red life,—that he may pass judgment on it: at any rate he will think it necessary to be a living man himself, before he can believe in his power of judging. And this is the title of the modern philosophers to sit among the great aiders of Life (or rather of the will to live), and the reason why they can look from their own out-wearied time and aspire to a truer culture, and a clearer explanation. Their yearning is, however, their danger ; the reformer in them struggles with the critical philosopher. And whichever way the victory incline, it also implies a defeat. How was Schopenhauer to escape this danger ?

We like to consider the great man as the noble child of his age, who feels its defects more strongly and intimately than the smaller men : and therefore the struggle of the great man *against* his age is apparently nothing but a mad fight to the death with himself. Only apparently, however : he only fights the elements in his time that hinder his own greatness, in other words his own freedom and sincerity. And so, at bottom, he is only an enemy to that element which is not truly himself, the irreconcilable antagonism of the temporal and eternal in him. The supposed "child of his age" proves to be but a step-child. From boyhood Schopenhauer strove with his time, a false and unworthy mother to him, and as soon as he had banished her, he could bring back his being to its native health and purity. For this very reason we can use his writings as mirrors of his time; it is no fault of the mirror if everything contemporary appear in it stricken by a ravaging disease, pale and thin, with tired looks and hollow eyes,—the step-child's sorrow made visible. The yearning for natural strength, for a healthy and simple humanity, was a yearning for himself: and as soon as he had conquered his time within him, he was face to face with his own genius. The secret of nature's being and his own lay open, the step-mother's plot to conceal his genius from him was foiled. And now he could turn a fearless eye towards the question, "What is the real worth of life?" without having any more to weigh a blood-less and chaotic age of doubt and hypocrisy. He knew that there was something higher and purer to be won on this earth than the life of his time, and a man does bitter wrong to existence who only knows it and criticises it in this hateful form. Genius, itself the highest product of life, is now summoned to justify life, if it can: the noble creative soul must answer the question:—"Dost thou in thy heart say 'Yea!' unto this existence? Is it enough for thee? Wilt thou be its advocate and its redeemer? One true 'Yea' from thy lips,

and the sorely accused life shall go free." How
shall he answer? In the words of Empedocles.

IV.

The last hint may well remain obscure for a
time: I have something more easy to explain,
namely how Schopenhauer can help us to educate
ourselves *in opposition to* our age, since we have
the advantage of really knowing our age, through
him ;—if it be an advantage! It may be no longer
possible in a couple of hundred years. I sometimes amuse myself with the idea that men may
soon grow tired of books and their authors, and
the savant of to-morrow come to leave directions
in his will that his body be burned in the midst of
his books, including of course his own writings.
And in the gradual clearing of the forests, might
not our libraries be very reasonably used for straw
and brushwood? Most books are born from the
smoke and vapour of the brain: and to vapour and
smoke may they well return. For having no fire
within themselves, they shall be visited with fire.
And possibly to a later century our own may count
as the " Dark age," because our productions heated
the furnace hotter and more continuously than
ever before. We are anyhow happy that we can
learn to know our time; and if there be any sense
in busying ourselves with our time at all, we may
as well do it as thoroughly as we can, so that no
one may have any doubt about it. The possibility
of this we owe to Schopenhauer.

Our happiness would of course be infinitely greater, if our inquiry showed that nothing so hopeful and splendid as our present epoch had ever existed. There are simple people in some corner of the earth to-day—perhaps in Germany— who are disposed to believe in all seriousness that the world was put right two years ago,* and that all stern and gloomy views of life are now con- tradicted by "facts." The foundation of the New German Empire is, to them, the decisive blow that annihilates all the "pessimistic" philosophisers,— no doubt of it. To judge the philosopher's signifi- cance in our time, as an educator, we must oppose a widespread view like this, especially common in our universities. We must say, it is a shameful thing that such abominable flattery of the Time- Fetish should be uttered by a herd of so-called reflective and honourable men ; it is a proof that we no longer see how far the seriousness of philosophy is removed from that of a newspaper. Such men have lost the last remnant of feeling, not only for philosophy, but also for religion, and have put in its place a spirit not so much of optimism as of journalism, the evil spirit that broods over the day—and the daily paper. Every philosophy that believes the problem of existence to be shelved, or even solved, by a political event, is a sham philosophy. There have been innumerable states founded since the beginning of the world ; that is an old story. How should a political innovation manage once and for all to make a contented race

---

* This was written in 1873.—Tr.

of the dwellers on this earth? If any one believe in his heart that this is possible, he should report himself to our authorities: he really deserves to be Professor of Philosophy in a German university, like Harms in Berlin, Jürgen Meyer in Bonn, and Carrière in Munich.

We are feeling the consequences of the doctrine, preached lately from all the housetops, that the state is the highest end of man and there is no higher duty than to serve it: I regard this not a relapse into paganism, but into stupidity. A man who thinks state-service to be his highest duty, very possibly knows no higher one; yet there are both men and duties in a region beyond,—and one of these duties, that seems to me at least of higher value than state-service, is to destroy stupidity in all its forms—and this particular stupidity among them. And I have to do with a class of men whose teleological conceptions extend further than the well-being of a state, I mean with philosophers —and only with them in their relation to the world of culture, which is again almost independent of the " good of the state." Of the many links that make up the twisted chain of humanity, some are of gold and others of pewter.

How does the philosopher of our time regard culture? Quite differently, I assure you, from the professors who are so content with their new state. He seems to see the symptoms of an absolute uprooting of culture in the increasing rush and hurry of life, and the decay of all reflection and simplicity. The waters of religion are ebbing, and leaving swamps or stagnant pools: the nations are

drawing away in enmity again, and long to tear
each other in pieces. The sciences, blindly driving along, on a *laisser faire* system, without a
common standard, are splitting up, and losing hold
of every firm principle. The educated classes are
being swept along in the contemptible struggle for
wealth. Never was the world more worldly, never
poorer in goodness and love. Men of learning are
no longer beacons or sanctuaries in the midst of
this turmoil of worldliness; they themselves are
daily becoming more restless, thoughtless, loveless.
Everything bows before the coming barbarism, art
and science included. The educated men have
degenerated into the greatest foes of education, for
they will deny the universal sickness and hinder
the physician. They become peevish, these poor
nerveless creatures, if one speak of their weakness
and combat the shameful spirit of lies in them.
They would gladly make one believe that they
have outstripped all the centuries, and they walk
with a pretence of happiness which has something
pathetic about it, because their happiness is so
inconceivable. One would not even ask them, as
Tannhäuser did Biterolf, "What hast thou, poor
wretch, enjoyed!" For, alas! we know far better
ourselves, in another way. There is a wintry sky
over us, and we dwell on a high mountain, in
danger and in need. Short-lived is all our joy,
and the sun's rays strike palely on our white
mountains. Music is heard; an old man grinds
an organ, and the dancers whirl round, and the
heart of the wanderer is shaken within him to see
it: everything is so disordered, so drab, so hope-

less. Even now there is a sound of joy, of clear
thoughtless joy! but soon the mist of evening
closes round, the note dies away, and the wanderer's
footsteps are heard on the gravel; as far as his
eye can reach there is nothing but the grim and
desolate face of nature.

It may be one-sided, to insist only on the blurred
lines and the dull colours in the picture of modern
life: yet the other side is no more encouraging,
it is only more disturbing. There is certainly
strength there, enormous strength; but it is wild,
primitive and merciless. One looks on with a
chill expectancy, as though into the caldron of a
witch's kitchen; every moment there may arise
sparks and vapour, to herald some fearful appari-
tion. For a century we have been ready for a
world-shaking convulsion; and though we have
lately been trying to set the conservative strength
of the so-called national state against the great
modern tendency to volcanic destructiveness, it
will only be, for a long time yet, an aggravation
of the universal unrest that hangs over us. We
need not be deceived by individuals behaving as if
they knew nothing of all this anxiety: their own
restlessness shows how well they know it. They
think more exclusively of themselves than men
ever thought before; they plant and build for their
little day, and the chase for happiness is never
greater than when the quarry must be caught to-
day or to-morrow: the next day perhaps there is
no more hunting. We live in the Atomic Age, or
rather in the Atomic Chaos. The opposing forces
were practically held together in mediæval times

by the Church, and in some measure assimilated by the strong pressure which she exerted. When the common tie broke and the pressure relaxed, they rose once more against each other. The Reformation taught that many things were "adiaphora"—departments that needed no guidance from religion: this was the price paid for its own existence. Christianity paid a similar one to guard itself against the far more religious antiquity: and laid the seeds of discord at once. Everything nowadays is directed by the fools and the knaves, the selfishness of the money-makers and the brute forces of militarism. The state in their hands makes a good show of reorganising everything, and of becoming the bond that unites the warring elements; in other words, it wishes for the same idolatry from mankind as they showed to the Church.

And we shall yet feel the consequences. We are even now on the ice-floes in the stream of the Middle Ages: they are thawing fast, and their movement is ominous: the banks are flooded, and giving way. The revolution, the atomistic revolution, is inevitable: but what *are* those smallest indivisible elements of human society?

There is surely far more danger to mankind in transitional periods like these than in the actual time of revolution and chaos; they are tortured by waiting, and snatch greedily at every moment; and this breeds all kinds of cowardice and selfishness in them: whereas the true feeling of a great and universal need ever inspires men, and makes them better. In the midst of such dangers, who

will provide the guardians and champions for
Humanity, for the holy and inviolate treasure that
has been laid up in the temples, little by little, by
countless generations?   Who will set up again
the *Image of Man*, when men in their selfishness
and terror see nothing but the trail of the serpent
or the cur in them, and have fallen from their high
estate to that of the brute or the automaton?

There are three Images of Man fashioned by our
modern time, which for a long while yet will urge
mortal men to transfigure their own lives; they
are the men of Rousseau, Goethe, and Schopenhauer.   The first has the greatest fire, and is most
calculated to impress the people: the second is
only for the few, for those contemplative natures
"in the grand style" who are misunderstood by
the crowd.   The third demands the highest activity
in those who will follow it: only such men will
look on that image without harm, for it breaks
the spirit of that merely contemplative man, and
the rabble shudder at it.   From the first has come
forth a strength that led and still leads to fearful
revolution: for in all socialistic upheavals it is ever
Rousseau's man who is the Typhoeus under the
Etna.   Oppressed and half crushed to death by
the pride of caste and the pitilessness of wealth,
spoilt by priests and bad education, a laughing-
stock even to himself, man cries in his need on
"holy mother Nature," and feels suddenly that she
is as far from him as any god of the Epicureans.
His prayers do not reach her; so deeply sunk is
he in the Chaos of the unnatural.   He contemptuously throws aside all the finery that seemed his

truest humanity a little while ago—all his arts
and sciences, all the refinements of his life,—he
beats with his fists against the walls, in whose
shadow he has degenerated, and goes forth to seek
the light and the sun, the forest and the crag.
And crying out, "Nature alone is good, the natural
man alone is human," he despises himself and
aspires beyond himself: a state wherein the soul
is ready for a fearful resolve, but calls the noble
and the rare as well from their utter depths.

Goethe's man is no such threatening force; in
a certain sense he is a corrective and a sedative to
those dangerous agitations of which Rousseau's
man is a prey.   Goethe himself in his youth
followed the "gospel of kindly Nature" with all
the ardour of his soul: his Faust was the highest
and boldest picture of Rousseau's man, so far at
any rate as his hunger for life, his discontent and
yearning, his intercourse with the demons of the
heart could be represented.   But what comes from
these congregated storm-clouds?   Not a single
lightning flash!   And here begins the new Image
of man—the man according to Goethe.   One
might have thought that Faust would have lived
a continual life of suffering, as a revolutionary and
a deliverer, as the negative force that proceeds
from goodness, as the genius of ruin, alike religious
and dæmonic, in opposition to his utterly un-
dæmonic companion; though of course he could
not be free of this companion, and had at once to
use and despise his evil and destructive scepticism
—which is the tragic destiny of all revolutionary
deliverers.   One is wrong, however, to expect

anything of the sort: Goethe's man here parts
company with Rousseau's; for he hates all violence,
all sudden transition—that is, all action: and the
universal deliverer becomes merely the universal
traveller. All the riches of life and nature, all
antiquity—arts, mythologies and sciences—pass
before his eager eyes, his deepest desires are
aroused and satisfied, Helen herself can hold him
no more—and the moment must come for which
his mocking companion is waiting. At a fair spot
on the earth, his flight comes to an end: his pinions
drop, and Mephistopheles is at his side. When
the German ceases to be Faust, there is no danger
greater than of becoming a Philistine and falling
into the hands of the devil—heavenly powers alone
can save him. Goethe's man is, as I said, the contemplative man in the grand style, who is only
kept from dying of ennui by feeding on all the
great and memorable things that have ever existed,
and by living from desire to desire. He is not the
active man; and when he does take a place among
active men, as things are, you may be sure that no
good will come of it (think, for example, of the zeal
with which Goethe wrote for the stage!); and
further, you may be sure that "things as they are"
will suffer no change. Goethe's man is a con-
ciliatory and conservative spirit, though in danger
of degenerating into a Philistine, just as Rousseau's
man may easily become a Catiline. All his virtues
would be the better by the addition of a little brute
force and elemental passion. Goethe appears to
have seen where the weakness and danger of his
creation lay, as is clear from Jarno's word to

Wilhelm Meister: "You are bitter and ill-tempered
—which is quite an excellent thing: if you could
once become really angry, it would be still better."

To speak plainly, it is necessary to become really
angry in order that things may be better. The
picture of Schopenhauer's man can help us here.
*Schopenhauer's man voluntarily takes upon himself
the pain of telling the truth:* this pain serves to
quench his individual will and make him ready for
the complete transformation of his being, which it
is the inner meaning of life to realise. This open-
ness in him appears to other men to be an effect
of malice, for they think the preservation of their
shifts and pretences to be the first duty of humanity,
and any one who destroys their playthings to be
merely malicious. They are tempted to cry out to
such a man, in Faust's words to Mephistopheles:—

> " So to the active and eternal
>   Creative force, in cold disdain
>   You now oppose the fist infernal "—

and he who would live according to Schopenhauer
would seem to be more like a Mephistopheles than
a Faust—that is, to our weak modern eyes, which
always discover signs of malice in any negation.
But there is a kind of denial and destruction that
is the effect of that strong aspiration after holiness
and deliverance, which Schopenhauer was the first
philosopher to teach our profane and worldly generation. Everything that can be denied, deserves to
be denied; and real sincerity means the belief in
a state of things which cannot be denied, or in
which there is no lie. The sincere man feels that

his activity has a metaphysical meaning. It can only be explained by the laws of a different and a higher life; it is in the deepest sense an affirmation: even if everything that he does seem utterly opposed to the laws of our present life. It must lead therefore to constant suffering; but he knows, as Meister Eckhard did, that "the quickest beast that will carry you to perfection is suffering." Every one, I should think, who has such an ideal before him, must feel a wider sympathy; and he will have a burning desire to beccme a "Schopenhauer man";—pure and wonderfully patient, on his intellectual side full of a devouring fire, and far removed from the cold and contemptuous "neutrality" of the so-called scientific man; so high above any warped and morose outlook on life as to offer himself as the first victim of the truth he has won, with a deep consciousness of the sufferings that must spring from his sincerity. His courage will destroy his happiness on earth, he must be an enemy to the men he loves and the institutions in which he grew up, he must spare neither person nor thing, however it may hurt him, he will be misunderstood and thought an ally of forces that he abhors, in his search for righteousness he will seem unrighteous by human standards: but he must comfort himself with the words that his teacher Schopenhauer once used: "A happy life is impossible, the highest thing that man can aspire to is a *heroic* life; such as a man lives, who is always fighting against unequal odds for the good of others; and wins in the end without any thanks. After the battle is over, he stands like

the Prince in the *re corvo* of Gozzi, with dignity
and nobility in his eyes, but turned to stone. His
memory remains, and will be reverenced as a
hero's ; his will, that has been mortified all his life
by toiling and struggling, by evil payment and
ingratitude, is absorbed into Nirvana." Such a
heroic life, with its full " mortification "—corresponds very little to the paltry ideas of the people
who talk most about it, and make festivals in
memory of great men, in the belief that a great
man is great in the sense that they are small,
either through exercise of his gifts to please himself
or by a blind mechanical obedience to this inner
force; so that the man who does not possess the
gift or feel the compulsion has the same right to
be small as the other to be great. But " gift " and
" compulsion " are contemptible words, mere means
of escape from an inner voice, a slander on him
who has listened to the voice—the great man ; he
least of all will allow himself to be given or compelled to anything: for he knows as well as any
smaller man how easily life can be taken and how
soft the bed whereon he might lie if he went the
pleasant and conventional way with himself and
his fellow-creatures : all the regulations of mankind
are turned to the end that the intense feeling of
life may be lost in continual distractions. Now
why will he so strongly choose the opposite, and
try to feel life, which is the same as to suffer from
life ? Because he sees that men will tempt him to
betray himself, and that there is a kind of agree-
ment to draw him from his den. He will prick
up his ears and gather himself together, and say,

"I will remain mine own." He gradually comes to understand what a fearful decision it is. For he must go down into the depths of being, with a string of curious questions on his lips—"Why am I alive? what lesson have I to learn from life? how have I become what I am, and why do I suffer in this existence?" He is troubled, and sees that no one is troubled in the same way; but rather that the hands of his fellow-men are passionately stretched out towards the fantastic drama of the political theatre, or they themselves are treading the boards under many disguises, youths, men and graybeards, fathers, citizens, priests, merchants and officials,—busy with the comedy they are all playing, and never thinking of their own selves. To the question "To what end dost thou live?" they would all immediately answer, with pride, "To *become* a good citizen or professor or statesman,"—and yet they *are* something which can never be changed: and why are they just—this? Ah, and why nothing better? The man who only regards his life as a moment in the evolution of a race or a state or a science, and will belong merely to a history of "becoming," has not understood the lesson of existence, and must learn it over again. This eternal "becoming something" is a lying puppet-show, in which man has forgot himself; it is the force that scatters individuality to the four winds, the eternal childish game that the big baby time is playing in front of us—and with us. The heroism of sincerity lies in ceasing to be the plaything of time. Everything in the process of "becoming" is a hollow sham, contemptible and

shallow : man can only find the solution of his
riddle in " being " something definite and unchangeable.   He begins to test how deep both " becoming "
and " being " are rooted in him—and a fearful task
is before his soul ; to destroy the first, and bring
all the falsity of things to the light.   He wishes to
know everything, not to feed a delicate taste, like
Goethe's man, to take delight, from a safe place,
in the multiplicity of existence : but he himself is
the first sacrifice that he brings.   The heroic man
does not think of his happiness or misery, his
virtues or his vices, or of his being the measure of
things ; he has no further hopes of himself and
will accept the utter consequences of his hopelessness.   His strength lies in his self-forgetfulness :
if he have a thought for himself, it is only to
measure the vast distance between himself and his
aim, and to view what he has left behind him as
so much dross.   The old philosophers sought for
happiness and truth, with all their strength : and
there is an evil principle in nature that not one
shall find that which he cannot help seeking.   But
the man who looks for a lie in everything, and
becomes a willing friend to unhappiness, shall have
a marvellous disillusioning : there hovers near him
something unutterable, of which truth and happiness
are but idolatrous images born of the night ; the
earth loses her dragging weight, the events and
powers of earth become as a dream, and a gradual
clearness widens round him like a summer evening.
It is as though the beholder of these things began
to wake, and it had only been the clouds of a
passing dream that had been weaving about him.

They will at some time disappear: and then will it be day.

V.

But I have promised to speak of Schopenhauer, as far as my experience goes, as an *educator*, and it is far from being sufficient to paint the ideal humanity which is the " Platonic idea " in Schopenhauer; especially as my representation is an imperfect one.   The most difficult task remains;—to say how a new circle of duties may spring from this ideal, and how one can reconcile such a transcendent aim with ordinary action; to prove, in short, that the ideal is *educative*.   One might otherwise think it to be merely the blissful or intoxicating vision of a few rare moments, that leaves us afterwards the prey of a deeper disappointment.   It is certain that the ideal begins to affect us in this way when we come suddenly to distinguish light and darkness, bliss and abhorrence; this is an experience that is as old as ideals themselves.   But we ought not to stand in the doorway for long; we should soon leave the first stages, and ask the question, seriously and definitely, " Is it possible to bring that incredibly high aim so near us, that it should educate us, or ' lead us out,' as well as lead us upward ? "—in order that the great words of Goethe be not fulfilled in our case—" Man is born to a state of limitation : he can understand ends that are simple, present and definite, and is accustomed to make use of means that are near to his hand ; but as soon as he comes into the open,

he knows neither what he wishes nor what he ought
to do, and it is all one whether he be confused by
the multitude of objects or set beside himself by
their greatness and importance.   It is always his
misfortune to be led to strive after something which
he cannot attain by any ordinary activity of his
own." The objection can be made with apparent
reason against Schopenhauer's man, that his greatness and dignity can only turn our heads, and put
us beyond all community with the active men of
the world : the common round of duties, the noise-
less tenor of life has disappeared.   One man may
possibly get accustomed to living in a reluctant
dualism, that is, in a contradiction with himself;—
becoming unstable, daily weaker and less productive :—while another will renounce all action
on principle, and scarcely endure to see others
active.   The danger is always great when a man
is too heavy-laden, and cannot really *accomplish*
any duties.   Stronger natures may be broken by
it; the weaker, which are the majority, sink into
a speculative laziness, and at last, from their laziness, lose even the power of speculation.

With regard to such objections, I will admit that
our work has hardly begun, and so far as I know,
I only see one thing clearly and definitely—that it
is possible for that ideal picture to provide you and
me with a chain of duties that may be accomplished; and some of us already feel its pressure.
In order, however, to be able to speak in plain
language of the formula under which I may gather
the new circle of duties, I must begin with the
following considerations.

The deeper minds of all ages have had pity for animals, because they suffer from life and have not the power to turn the sting of the suffering against themselves, and understand their being metaphysically. The sight of blind suffering is the spring of the deepest emotion. And in many quarters of the earth men have supposed that the souls of the guilty have entered into beasts, and that the blind suffering which at first sight calls for such pity has a clear meaning and purpose to the divine justice,—of punishment and atonement: and a heavy punishment it is, to be condemned to live in hunger and need, in the shape of a beast, and to reach no consciousness of one's self in this life. I can think of no harder lot than the wild beast's; he is driven to the forest by the fierce pang of hunger, that seldom leaves him at peace; and peace is itself a torment, the surfeit after horrid food, won, maybe, by a deadly fight with other animals. To cling to life, blindly and madly, with no other aim, to be ignorant of the reason, or even the fact, of one's punishment, nay, to thirst after it as if it were a pleasure, with all the perverted desire of a fool—this is what it means to be an animal. If universal nature leads up to man, it is to show us that he is necessary to redeem her from the curse of the beast's life, and that in him existence can find a mirror of itself wherein life appears, no longer blind, but in its real metaphysical significance. But we should consider where the beast ends and the man begins—the man, the one concern of Nature. As long as any one desires life as a pleasure in itself, he has not raised his eyes above

the horizon of the beast; he only desires more
consciously what the beast seeks by a blind impulse.
It is so with us all, for the greater part of our lives.
We do not shake off the beast, but are beasts ourselves, suffering we know not what.

But there are moments when we do know; and
then the clouds break, and we see how, with the
rest of nature, we are straining towards the man,
as to something that stands high above us. We
look round and behind us, and fear the sudden
rush of light; the beasts are transfigured, and ourselves with them. The enormous migrations of
mankind in the wildernesses of the world, the cities
they found and the wars they wage, their ceaseless
gatherings and dispersions and fusions, the doctrines
they blindly follow, their mutual frauds and deceits,
the cry of distress, the shriek of victory—are all a
continuation of the beast in us: as if the education
of man has been intentionally set back, and his
promise of self-consciousness frustrated; as if, in
fact, after yearning for man so long, and at last
reaching him by her labour, Nature should now
recoil from him and wish to return to a state
of unconscious instinct. Ah! she has need of
knowledge, and shrinks before the very knowledge
she needs: the flame flickers unsteadily and fears
its own brightness, and takes hold of a thousand
things before the one thing for which knowledge
is necessary. There are moments when we all
know that our most elaborate arrangements are
only designed to give us refuge from our real
task in life; we wish to hide our heads somewhere,
as if our Argus-eyed conscience could not find us

out; we are quick to send our hearts on state-service, or money-making, or social duties, or scientific work, in order to possess them no longer ourselves; we are more willing and instinctive slaves of the hard day's work than mere living requires, because it seems to us more necessary not to be in a position to think. The hurry is universal, because every one is fleeing before himself; its concealment is just as universal, as we wish to seem contented and hide our wretchedness from the keener eyes; and so there is a common need for a new carillon of words to hang in the temple of life, and peal for its noisy festival. We all know the curious way in which unpleasant memories suddenly throng on us, and how we do our best by loud talk and violent gestures to put them out of our minds; but the gestures and the talk of our ordinary life make one think we are all in this condition, frightened of any memory or any inward gaze. What is it that is always troubling us? what is the gnat that will not let us sleep? There are spirits all about us, each moment of life has something to say to us, but we will not listen to the spirit-voices. When we are quiet and alone, we fear that something will be whispered in our ears, and so we hate the quiet, and dull our senses in society.

We understand this sometimes, as I say, and stand amazed at the whirl and the rush and the anxiety and all the dream that we call our life; we seem to fear the awakening, and our dreams too become vivid and restless, as the awakening draws near. But we feel as well that we are too weak to endure long those intimate moments, and that we are not the men to whom universal nature looks as her redeemers. It is something to be able to raise our heads but for a moment and see the stream in which we are sunk so deep. We cannot gain even this transitory moment of awakening by our own strength; we must be lifted up—and who are they that will uplift us?

The sincere men who have cast out the beast, the philosophers, artists and saints. Nature—*quæ nunquam facit saltum*—has made her one leap in creating them; a leap of joy, as she feels herself for the first time at her goal, where she begins to see that she must learn not to have goals above her, and that she has played the game of transition too long. The knowledge transfigures her, and there rests on her face the gentle weariness of evening that men call "beauty." Her words after this transfiguration are as a great light shed over existence: and the highest wish that mortals can reach is to listen continually to her voice with ears that hear. If a man think of all that Schopenhauer, for example, must have *heard* in his life, he may well say to himself—"The deaf ears, the feeble understanding and shrunken heart, everything that I call mine,—how I despise them! Not to be able to fly but only to flutter one's wings! To look above one's self and have no power to rise! To know the road that leads to the wide vision of the philosopher, and to reel back after a few steps! Were there but one day when the great wish might be fulfilled, how gladly would we pay for it with the rest of life! To rise as high as any thinker yet into the pure icy air of the mountain, where there are no mists and veils, and the inner constitution of things is shown in a stark and piercing clarity! Even by thinking of this the soul becomes infinitely alone ; but were its wish fulfilled, did its glance once fall straight as a ray of light on the things below, were shame and anxiety and desire gone for ever—one could find no words for its state then, for the mystic and tranquil emotion with which, like the soul of Schopenhauer, it would look down on the monstrous hieroglyphics of existence and the petrified doctrines of " becoming "; not as the brooding night, but as the red and glowing day that streams over the earth. And what a destiny it is only to know enough of the fixity and happiness of the philosopher to feel the complete unfixity and unhappiness of the false philosopher, ' who without hope lives in desire ': to know one's self to be the fruit of a tree that is too much in the shade ever to ripen, and to see a world of sunshine in front, where one may not go ! "

There were sorrow enough here, if ever, to make such a man envious and spiteful: but he will turn aside, that he may not destroy his soul by a vain aspiration ; and will discover a new circle of duties.

I can now give an answer to the question whether it be possible to approach the great ideal of Schopenhauer's man " by any ordinary activity of our own." In the first place, the new duties are certainly not those of a hermit ; they imply rather a vast community, held together not by external forms but by a fundamental idea, namely that of *culture* ;

though only so far as it can put a single task
before each of us—to bring the philosopher, the
artist and the saint, within and without us, to the
light, and to strive thereby for the completion of
Nature. For Nature needs the artist, as she needs
the philosopher, for a metaphysical end, the
explanation of herself, whereby she may have a
clear and sharp picture of what she only saw
dimly in the troubled period of transition,—and
so may reach self-consciousness. Goethe, in an
arrogant yet profound phrase, showed how all
Nature's attempts only have value in so far as the
artist interprets her stammering words, meets her
half-way, and speaks aloud what she really means.
" I have often said, and will often repeat," he
exclaims in one place, " the *causa finalis* of natural
and human activity is dramatic poetry. Otherwise the stuff is of no use at all."

Finally, Nature needs the saint. In him the
ego has melted away, and the suffering of his life
is, practically, no longer felt as individual, but as
the spring of the deepest sympathy and intimacy
with all living creatures: he sees the wonderful
transformation scene that the comedy of " becoming " never reaches, the attainment, at length, of
the high state of man after which all nature is
striving, that she may be delivered from herself.
Without doubt, we all stand in close relation to
him, as well as to the philosopher and the artist:
there are moments, sparks from the clear fire of
love, in whose light we understand the word " I "
no longer; there is something beyond our being
that comes, for those moments, to the hither side

of it: and this is why we long in our hearts for a bridge from here to there. In our ordinary state we can do nothing towards the production of the new redeemer, and so we hate ourselves in this state with a hatred that is the root of the pessimism which Schopenhauer had to teach again to our age, though it is as old as the aspiration after culture. —Its root, not its flower; the foundation, not the summit; the beginning of the road, not the end: for we have to learn at some time to hate something else, more universal than our own personality with its wretched limitation, its change and its unrest—and this will be when we shall learn to love something else than we can love now. When we are ourselves received into that high order of philosophers, artists and saints, in this life or a reincarnation of it, a new object for our love and hate will also rise before us. As it is, we have our task and our circle of duties, our hates and our loves. For we know that culture requires us to make ready for the coming of the Schopenhauer man;—and this is the " use " we are to make of him;—we must know what obstacles there are and strike them from our path—in fact, wage unceasing war against everything that hindered our fulfilment, and prevented us from becoming Schopenhauer's men ourselves.

VI.

It is sometimes harder to agree to a thing than to understand it; many will feel this when they consider the proposition—" Mankind must toil

unceasingly to bring forth individual great men:
this and nothing else is its task." One would like
to apply to society and its ends a fact that holds
universally in the animal and vegetable world;
where progress depends only on the higher individual types, which are rarer, yet more persistent, complex and productive. But traditional
notions of what the end of society is, absolutely
bar the way. We can easily understand how in
the natural world, where one species passes at
some point into a higher one, the aim of their
evolution cannot be held to lie in the high level
attained by the mass, or in the latest types
developed;—but rather in what seem accidental
beings produced here and there by favourable
circumstances. It should be just as easy to
understand that it is the duty of mankind to
provide the circumstances favourable to the birth
of the new redeemer, simply because men can
have a consciousness of their object. But there
is always something to prevent them. They find
their ultimate aim in the happiness of all, or the
greatest number, or in the expansion of a great
commonwealth. A man will very readily decide
to sacrifice his life for the state; he will be much
slower to respond if an individual, and not a state,
ask for the sacrifice. It seems to be out of reason
that one man should exist for the sake of another:
" Let it be rather for the sake of every other, or,
at any rate, of as many as possible!" O upright
judge! As if it were more in reason to let the
majority decide a question of value and significance! For the problem is—" In what way may

your life, the individual life, retain the highest
value and the deepest significance? and how may
it least be squandered?"   Only by your living for
the good of the rarest and most valuable types,
not for that of the majority,—who are the most
worthless types, taken as individuals.   This way
of thinking should be implanted and fostered in
every young man's mind: he should regard himself
both as a failure of Nature's handiwork and a
testimony to her larger ideas.   "She has succeeded
badly," he should say; "but I will do honour to
her great idea by being a means to its better
success."

With these thoughts he will enter the circle
of culture, which is the child of every man's self-
knowledge and dissatisfaction.   He will approach
and say aloud: "I see something above me, higher
and more human than I: let all help me to reach
it, as I will help all who know and suffer as I do,
that the man may arise at last who feels his
knowledge and love, vision and power, to be
complete and boundless, who in his universality
is one with nature, the critic and judge of existence."   It is difficult to give any one this courageous
self-consciousness, because it is impossible to teach
love; from love alone the soul gains, not only the
clear vision that leads to self-contempt, but also
the desire to look to a higher self which is yet
hidden, and strive upward to it with all its strength.
And so he who rests his hope on a future great
man, receives his first "initiation into culture."
The sign of this is shame or vexation at one's self,
a hatred of one's own narrowness, a sympathy with

the genius that ever raises its head again from our
misty wastes, a feeling for all that is struggling
into life, the conviction that Nature must be helped
in her hour of need to press forward to the man,
however ill she seem to prosper, whatever success
may attend her marvellous forms and projects :
so that the men with whom we live are like the
débris of some precious sculptures, which cry out—
" Come and help us ! Put us together, for we long
to become complete."

I called this inward condition the " first initiation into culture." I have now to describe the
effects of the " second initiation," a task of greater
difficulty. It is the passage from the inner life to
the criticism of the outer life. The eye must be
turned to find in the great world of movement the
desire for culture that is known from the immediate
experience of the individual ; who must use his
own strivings and aspirations as the alphabet to
interpret those of humanity. [He cannot rest here
either, but must go higher. Culture demands from
him not only that inner experience, not only the
criticism of the outer world surrounding him, but
action too to crown them all, the fight for culture
against the influences and conventions and institutions where he cannot find his own aim,—the
production of genius.]

Any one who can reach the second step, will
see how extremely rare and imperceptible the
knowledge of that end is, though all men busy
themselves with culture and expend vast labour
in her service. He asks himself in amazement—
" Is not such knowledge, after all, absolutely

necessary? Can Nature be said to attain her
end, if men have a false idea of the aim of their
own labour?" And any one who thinks a great
deal of Nature's unconscious adaptation of means
to ends, will probably answer at once: "Yes, men
may think and speak what they like about their
ultimate end, their blind instinct will tell them the
right road." It requires some experience of life
to be able to contradict this: but let a man be
convinced of the real aim of culture—the production of the true man and nothing else;—let
him consider that amid all the pageantry and
ostentation of culture at the present time the
conditions for his production are nothing but a
continual "battle of the beasts": and he will see
that there is great need for a conscious will to take
the place of that blind instinct. There is another
reason also;—to prevent the possibility of turning
this obscure impulse to quite different ends, in a
direction where our highest aim can no longer be
attained. For we must beware of a certain kind
of misapplied and parasitical culture; the powers
at present most active in its propagation have
other casts of thought that prevent their relation
to culture from being pure and disinterested.

The first of these is the self-interest of the
business men. This needs the help of culture,
and helps her in return, though at the price of
prescribing her ends and limits. And their favourite
sorites is: "We must have as much knowledge
and education as possible; this implies as great
a need as possible for it, this again as much production, this again as much material wealth and

happiness as possible."—This is the seductive
formula. Its preachers would define education as
the insight that makes man through and through
a "child of his age" in his desires and their
satisfaction, and gives him command over the
best means of making money. Its aim would
be to make "current" men, in the same sense as
one speaks of the "currency" in money; and in
their view, the more "current" men there are,
the happier the people. The object of modern
educational systems is therefore to make each
man as "current" as his nature will allow him,
and to give him the opportunity for the greatest
amount of success and happiness that can be got
from his particular stock of knowledge. He is
required to have just so much idea of his own
value (through his liberal education) as to know
what he can ask of life; and he is assured that
a natural and necessary connection between
"intelligence and property" not only exists, but
is also a *moral* necessity. All education is de-
tested that makes for loneliness, and has an aim
above money-making, and requires a long time:
men look askance on such serious education, as
mere "refined egoism" or "immoral Epicurean-
ism." The converse of course holds, according
to the ordinary morality, that education must be
soon over to allow the pursuit of money to be
soon begun, and should be just thorough enough
to allow of much money being made. The amount of
education is determined by commercial interests. In
short, "man has a necessary claim to worldly happiness; only for that reason is education necessary."

There is, secondly, the self-interest of the state, which requires the greatest possible breadth and universality of culture, and has the most effective weapons to carry out its wishes. If it be firmly enough established not only to initiate but control education and bear its whole weight, such breadth will merely profit the competition of the state with other states. A " highly civilised state" generally implies, at the present time, the task of setting free the spiritual forces of a generation just so far as they may be of use to the existing institutions,— as a mountain stream is split up by embankments and channels, and its diminished power made to drive mill-wheels, its full strength being more dangerous than useful to the mills. And thus " setting free" comes to mean rather " chaining up." Compare, for example, what the self-interest of the state has done for Christianity. Christianity is one of the purest manifestations of the impulse towards culture and the production of the saint: but being used in countless ways to turn the mills of the state authorities, it gradually became sick at heart, hypocritical and degenerate, and in antagonism with its original aim. Its last phase, the German Reformation, would have been nothing but a sudden flickering of its dying flame, had it not taken new strength and light from the clash and conflagration of states.

In the third place, culture will be favoured by all those people who know their own character to be offensive or tiresome, and wish to draw a veil of so-called " good form" over them. Words, gestures, dress, etiquette, and such external things,

are meant to produce a false impression, the inner
side to be judged from the outer. I sometimes
think that modern men are eternally bored with
each other and look to the arts to make them
interesting. They let their artists make savoury
and inviting dishes of them ; they steep themselves
in the spices of the East and West, and have a
very interesting aroma after it all. They are ready
to suit all palates : and every one will be served,
whether he want something with a good or bad
taste, something sublime or coarse, Greek or
Chinese, tragedy or gutter - drama. The most
celebrated chefs among the moderns who wish to
interest and be interested at any price, are the
French ; the worst are the Germans. This is
really more comforting for the latter, and we have
no reason to mind the French despising us for our
want of interest, elegance and politeness, and being
reminded of the Indian who longs for a ring
through his nose, and then proceeds to tattoo
himself.

Here I must digress a little. Many things in
Germany have evidently been altered since the
late war with France, and new requirements for
German culture brought over. The war was for
many their first venture into the more elegant half
of the world : and what an admirable simplicity
the conqueror shows in not scorning to learn something of culture from the conquered ! The applied
arts especially will be reformed to emulate our more
refined neighbours, the German house furnished
like the French, a "sound taste" applied to the
German language by means of an Academy on the

French model, to shake off the doubtful influence of Goethe—this is the judgment of our new Berlin Academician, Dubois-Raymond. Our theatres have been gradually moving, in a dignified way, towards the same goal, even the elegant German savant is now discovered — and we must now expect everything that does not conform to this law of elegance, our music, tragedy and philosophy to be thrust aside as un-German. But there were no need to raise a finger for German culture, did German culture (which the Germans have yet to find) mean nothing but the little amenities that make life more decorative—including the arts of the dancing-master and the upholsterer;—or were they merely interested in academic rules of language and a general atmosphere of politeness. The late war and the self-comparison with the French do not seem to have aroused any further desires, and I suspect that the German has a strong wish for the moment to be free of the old obligations laid on him by his wonderful gifts of seriousness and profundity. He would much rather play the buffoon and the monkey, and learn the arts that make life amusing. But the German spirit cannot be more dishonoured than by being treated as wax for any elegant mould.

And if, unfortunately, a good many Germans will allow themselves to be thus moulded, one must continually say to them, till at last they listen:— "The old German way is no longer yours: it was hard, rough, and full of resistance; but it is still the most valuable material—one which only the greatest modellers can work with, for they alone

are worthy to use it. What you have in you now
is a soft pulpy stuff: make what you will out of
it,—elegant dolls and interesting idols—Richard
Wagner's phrase will still hold good, 'The German
is awkward and ungainly when he wishes to be
polite; he is high above all others, when he begins
to take fire.'" All the elegant people have reason to
beware of this German fire; it may one day devour
them with all their wax dolls and idols.—The
prevailing love of "good form" in Germany may
have a deeper cause in the breathless seizing at
what the moment can give, the haste that plucks
the fruit too green, the race and the struggle that
cut the furrows in men's brows and stamp the same
mark on all their actions. As if there were a
poison in them that would not let them breathe,
they rush about in disorder, anxious slaves of the
"three m's," the moment, the mode and the mob:
they see too well their want of dignity and fitness,
and need a false elegance to hide their galloping
consumption. The fashionable desire of "good
form" is bound up with a loathing of man's inner
nature: the one is to conceal, the other to be concealed. Education means now the concealment
of man's misery and wickedness, his wild-beast
quarrels, his eternal greed, his shamelessness in
fruition. In pointing out the absence of a German
culture, I have often had the reproach flung at me:
"This absence is quite natural, for the Germans
have been too poor and modest up to now. Once
rich and conscious of themselves, our people will
have a culture too." Faith may often produce
happiness, yet *this* particular faith makes me un-

happy, for I feel that the culture whose future raises such hopes—the culture of riches, politeness, and elegant concealments—is the bitterest foe of that German culture in which I believe. Every one who has to live among Germans suffers from the dreadful grayness and apathy of their lives, their formlessness, torpor and clumsiness, still more their envy, secretiveness and impurity: he is troubled by their innate love of the false and the ignoble, their wretched mimicry and translation of a good foreign thing into a bad German one. But now that the feverish unrest, the quest of gain and success, the intense prizing of the moment, is added to it all, it makes one furious to think that all this sickness can never be cured, but only painted over, by such a "cult of the interesting." And this among a people that has produced a Schopenhauer and a Wagner! and will produce others, unless we are blindly deceiving ourselves; for should not their very existence be a guarantee that such forces are even now potential in the German spirit? Or will they be exceptions, the last inheritors of the qualities that were once called German? I can see nothing to help me here, and return to my main argument again, from which my doubts and anxieties have made me digress. I have not yet enumerated all the forces that help culture without recognising its end, the production of genius. Three have been named; the self-interest of business, of the state, and of those who draw the cloak of "good form" over them. There is fourthly the self-interest of science, and the peculiar nature of her servants—the learned.

Science has the same relation to wisdom as current morality to holiness: she is cold and dry, loveless, and ignorant of any deep feeling of dissatisfaction and yearning. She injures her servants in helping herself, for she impresses her own character on them and dries up their humanity. As long as we actually mean by culture the progress of science, she will pass by the great suffering man and harden her heart, for science only sees the problems of knowledge, and suffering is something alien and unintelligible to her world —though no less a problem for that!

If one accustom himself to put down every experience in a dialectical form of question and answer, and translate it into the language of " pure reason," he will soon wither up and rattle his bones like a skeleton. We all know it: and why is it that the young do not shudder at these skeletons of men, but give themselves blindly to science without motive or measure? It cannot be the so-called " impulse to truth ": for how could there be an impulse towards a pure, cold and objectless knowledge? The unprejudiced eye can see the real driving forces only too plainly. The vivisection of the professor has much to recommend it, as he himself is accustomed to finger and analyse all things—even the worthiest! To speak honestly, the savant is a complex of very various impulses and attractive forces—he is a base metal throughout.

Take first a strong and increasing desire for intellectual adventure, the attraction of the new and rare as against the old and tedious. Add to that a certain joy in nosing the trail of dialectic, and beating the cover where the old fox, Thought, lies hid ; the desire is not so much for truth as the chase of truth, and the chief pleasure is in surrounding and artistically killing it.   Add thirdly a love of contradiction whereby the personality is able to assert itself against all others : the battle's the thing, and the personal victory its aim,—truth only its pretext.   The impulse to discover " particular truths " plays a great part in the professor, coming from his submission to definite ruling persons, classes, opinions, churches, governments, for he feels it a profit to himself to bring truth to their side.

The following characteristics of the savant are less common, but still found.—Firstly, downrightness and a feeling for simplicity, very valuable if more than a mere awkwardness and inability to deceive, deception requiring some mother-wit.— (Actually, we may be on our guard against too obvious cleverness and resource, and doubt the man's sincerity.) — Otherwise this downrightness is generally of little value, and rarely of any use to knowledge, as it follows tradition and speaks the truth only in " adiaphora "; it being lazier to speak the truth here than ignore it.   Everything new means something to be unlearnt, and your downright man will respect the ancient dogmas and accuse the new evangelist of failing in the *sensus recti*.   There was a similar opposition, with probability and custom on its side,. to the theory of Copernicus.   The professor's frequent hatred of philosophy is principally a hatred of the long trains of reasoning and artificiality of the proofs. Ultimately the savants of every age have a fixed limit; beyond which ingenuity is not allowed, and everything suspected as a conspirator against honesty.

Secondly, a clear vision of near objects, combined with great shortsightedness for the distant and universal. The professor's range is generally very small, and his eye must be kept close to the object. To pass from a point already considered to another, he has to move his whole optical apparatus. He cuts a picture into small sections, like a man using an opera-glass in the theatre, and sees now a head, now a bit of the dress, but nothing as a whole. The single sections are never combined for him, he only infers their connection, and consequently has no strong general impression. He judges a literary work, for example, by certain paragraphs or sentences or errors, as he can do nothing more; he will be driven to see in an oil painting nothing but a mass of daubs.

Thirdly, a sober conventionality in his likes and dislikes. Thus he especially delights in history because he can put his own motives into the actions of the past. A mole is most comfortable in a mole-hill. He is on his guard against all ingenious and extravagant hypotheses; but digs up industriously all the commonplace motives of the past, because he feels in sympathy with them. He is generally quite incapable of understanding and valuing the rare or the uncommon, the great or the real.

Fourthly, a lack of feeling, which makes him

capable of vivisection. He knows nothing of the suffering that brings knowledge, and does not fear to tread where other men shudder. He is cold and may easily appear cruel. He is thought courageous, but he is not,—any more than the mule who does not feel giddiness.

Fifthly, diffidence, or a low estimate of himself. Though he live in a miserable alley of the world, he has no sense of sacrifice or surrender ; he appears often to know in his inmost heart that he is not a flying but a crawling creature. And this makes him seem even pathetic.

Sixthly, loyalty to his teachers and leaders. From his heart he wishes to help them, and knows he can do it best with the truth. He has a grateful disposition, for he has only gained admittance through them to the high hall of science ; he would never have entered by his own road. Any man to-day who can throw open a new province where his lesser disciples can work to some purpose, is famous at once ; so great is the crowd that presses after him. These grateful pupils are certainly a misfortune to their teacher, as they all imitate him ; his faults are exaggerated in their small persons, his virtues correspondingly diminished.

Seventhly, he will follow the usual road of all the professors, where a feeling for truth springs from a lack of ideas, and the wheel once started goes on. Such natures become compilers, commentators, makers of indices and herbaria; they rummage about one special department because they have never thought there are others. Their industry has something of the monstrous stupidity of gravitation; and so they can often bring their labours to an end.

Eighthly, a dread of ennui. While the true thinker desires nothing more than leisure, the professor fears it, not knowing how it is to be used. Books are his comfort; he listens to everybody's different thoughts and keeps himself amused all day. He especially chooses books with a personal relation to himself, that make him feel some emotion of like or dislike; books that have to do with himself or his position, his political, æsthetic, or even grammatical doctrines; if he have mastered even one branch of knowledge, the means to flap away the flies of ennui will not fail him.

Ninthly, the motive of the bread-winner, the "cry of the empty stomach," in fact. Truth is used as a direct means of preferment, when she can be attained; or as a way to the good graces of the fountains of honour — and bread. Only, however, in the sense of the "particular truth": there is a gulf between the profitable truths that many serve, and the unprofitable truths to which only those few people devote themselves whose motto is not *ingenii largitor venter*.

Tenthly, a reverence for their fellow-professors and a fear of their displeasure—a higher and rarer motive than the last, though not uncommon. All the members of the guild are jealously on guard, that the truth which means so much bread and honour and position may really be baptized in the name of its discoverer. The one pays the other reverence for the truth he has found, in order to exact the toll again if he should find one himself.

The Untruth, the Error is loudly exploded, that the workers may not be too many; here and there the real truth will be exploded to let a few bold and stiff-necked errors be on show for a time; there is never a lack of " moral idiosyncrasies,"—formerly called rascalities.

Eleventhly, the " savant for vanity," now rather rare. He will get a department for himself somehow, and investigate curiosities, especially if they demand unusual expenditure, travel, research, or communication with all parts of the world. He is quite satisfied with the honour of being regarded as a curiosity himself, and never dreams of earning a living by his erudite studies.

Twelfthly, the " savant for amusement." He loves to look for knots in knowledge and to untie them ; not too energetically however, lest he lose the spirit of the game. Thus he does not penetrate the depths, though he often observes something that the microscopic eyes of the bread-and-butter scientist never see.

If I speak, lastly, of the "impulse towards justice" as a further motive of the savant, I may be answered that this noble impulse, being metaphysical in its nature, is too indistinguishable from the rest, and really incomprehensible to mortal mind ; and so I leave the thirteenth heading with the pious wish that the impulse may be less rare in the professor than it seems. For a spark in his soul from the fire of justice is sufficient to irradiate and purify it, so that he can rest no more and is driven for ever from the cold or lukewarm condition in which most of his fellows do their daily work.

All these elements, or a part of them, must be regarded as fused and pounded together, to form the Servant of Truth. For the sake of an absolutely inhuman thing—mere purposeless, and therefore motiveless, knowledge—a mass of very human little motives have been chemically combined, and as the result we have the professor,—so transfigured in the light of that pure unearthly object that the mixing and pounding which went to form him are all forgotten! It is very curious. Yet there are moments when they must be remembered,—when we have to think of the professor's significance to culture. Any one with observation can see that he is in his essence and by his origin unproductive, and has a natural hatred of the productive; and thus there is an endless feud between the genius and the savant in idea and practice. The latter wishes to kill Nature by analysing and comprehending it, the former to increase it by a new living Nature. The happy age does not need or know the savant; the sick and sluggish time ranks him as its highest and worthiest.

Who were physician enough to know the health or sickness of our time? It is clear that the professor is valued too highly, with evil consequences for the future genius, for whom he has no compassion, merely a cold, contemptuous criticism, a shrug of the shoulders, as if at something strange and perverted for which he has neither time nor inclination. And so he too knows nothing of the aim of culture.

In fact, all these considerations go to prove that the aim of culture is most unknown precisely where the interest in it seems liveliest. The state may trumpet as it will its services to culture, it merely helps culture in order to help itself, and does not comprehend an aim that stands higher than its own well-being or even existence. The business men in their continual demand for education merely wish for—business. When the pioneers of "good form" pretend to be the real helpers of culture, imagining that all art, for example, is merely to serve their own needs, they are clearly affirming themselves in affirming culture. Of the savant enough has already been said. All four are emulously thinking how they can benefit *themselves* with the help of culture, but have no thoughts at all when their own interests are not engaged. And so they have done nothing to improve the conditions for the birth of genius in modern times ; and the opposition to original men has grown so far that no Socrates could ever live among us, and certainly could never reach the age of seventy.

I remember saying in the third chapter that our whole modern world was not so stable that one could prophesy an eternal life to its conception of culture. It is likely that the next millennium may reach two or three new ideas that might well make the hair of our present generation stand on end. The belief in the metaphysical significance of culture would not be such a horrifying thing, but its effects on educational methods might be so.

It requires a totally new attitude of mind to be able to look away from the present educational institutions to the strangely different ones that will be necessary for the second or third generation.

At present the labours of higher education produce merely the savant or the official or the business man or the Philistine or, more commonly, a mixture of all four; and the future institutions will have a harder task;—not in itself harder, as it is really more natural, and so easier; and further, could anything be harder than to make a youth into a savant against nature, as now happens?—But the difficulty lies in unlearning what we know and setting up a new aim; it will be an endless trouble to change the fundamental idea of our present educational system, that has its roots in the Middle Ages and regards the mediæval savant as the ideal type of culture. It is already time to put these objects before us; for some generation must begin the battle, of which a later generation will reap the victory. The solitary man who has understood the new fundamental idea of culture is at the parting of the ways; on the one he will be welcomed by his age, laurels and rewards will be his, powerful parties will uphold him, he will have as many in sympathy behind him as in front, and when the leader speaks the word of deliverance, it will echo through all the ranks. The first duty is to "fight in line," the second to treat as foes all who will not "fall in." On the other way he will find fewer companions; it is steeper and more tortuous. The travellers on the first road laugh at him, as his way is the more troublesome and dangerous; and they try to entice him over. If the two ways cross, he is ill-treated, cast aside or left alone. What significance has any particular form of culture for these several travellers? The enormous throng that press to their end on the first road, understand by it the laws and institutions that enable them to go forward in regular fashion and rule out all the solitary and obstinate people who look towards higher and remoter objects. To the small company on the other road it has quite a different office : they wish to guard themselves, by means of a strong organisation, from being swept away by the throng, to prevent their individual members from fainting on the way or turning in spirit from their great task. These solitary men must finish their work ; that is why they should all hold together ; and those who have their part in the scheme will take thought to prepare themselves with ever-increasing purity of aim for the birth of the genius, and ensure that the time be ripe for him. Many are destined to help on the labour, even among the second-rate talents, and it is only in submission to such a destiny that they can feel they are living for a duty, and have a meaning and an object in their lives. But at present these talents are being turned from the road their instinct has chosen by the seductive tones of the " fashionable culture," that plays on their selfish side, their vanities and weaknesses ; and the time-spirit ever whispers in their ears its flattering counsel :—" Follow me and go not thither ! There you are only servants and tools, overshadowed by higher natures with no scope for your own, drawn by threads, hung with fetters, slaves and automatons. With me you may enjoy your true personality, and be masters, your talents may shine with their own light, and yourselves stand in the front ranks with an immense following round you; and the acclamation of public opinion will rejoice you more than a wandering breath of approval sent down from the cold ethereal heights of genius." Even the best men are snared by such allurements, and the ultimate difference comes not so much from the rarity and power of their talent, as the influence of a certain heroic disposition at the base of them, and an inner feeling of kinship with genius. For there are men who feel it as their own misery when they see the genius in painful toil and struggle, in danger of self-destruction, or neglected by the short-sighted selfishness of the state, the superficiality of the business men, and the cold arrogance of the professors; and I hope there may be some to understand what I mean by my sketch of Schopenhauer's destiny, and to what end Schopenhauer can really educate.

VII.

But setting aside all thoughts of any educational revolution in the distant future;—what provision is required *now*, that our future philosopher may have the best chance of opening his eyes to a life like Schopenhauer's—hard as it is, yet still livable? What, further, must be discovered that may make his influence on his contemporaries more certain? And what obstacles must be removed before his example can have its full effect and the philosopher train another philosopher? Here we descend to be practical.

Nature always desires the greatest utility, but does not understand how to find the best and handiest means to her end ; that is her great sorrow, and the cause of her melancholy.   The impulse towards her own redemption shows clearly her wish to give men a significant existence by the generation of the philosopher and the artist : but how unclear and weak is the effect she generally obtains with her artists and philosophers, and how seldom is there any effect at all !   She is especially perplexed in her efforts to make the philosopher useful ; her methods are casual and tentative, her failures innumerable ; most of her philosophers never touch the common good of mankind at all.   Her actions seem those of a spendthrift ; but the cause lies in no prodigal luxury, but in her inexperience.   Were she human, she would probably never cease to be dissatisfied with herself and her bungling.   Nature shoots the philosopher at mankind like an arrow ; she does not aim, but hopes that the arrow will stick somewhere.   She makes countless mistakes, that give her pain.   She is as extravagant in the sphere of culture as in her planting and sowing.   She fulfils her ends in a large and clumsy fashion, using up far too much of her strength.   The artist has the same relation to the connoisseurs and lovers of his art as a piece of heavy artillery to a flock of sparrows.   It is a fool's part to use a great avalanche to sweep away a little snow, to kill a man in order to strike the fly on his nose.   The artist and the philosopher are witnesses against Nature's adaptation of her means, however well they may show the wisdom of her ends.   They only reach a few and should reach all—and even these few are not struck with the strength they used when they shot. It is sad to have to value art so differently as cause and effect; how huge in its inception, how faint the echo afterwards! The artist does his work as Nature bids him, for the benefit of other men—no doubt of it; but he knows that none of those men will understand and love his work as he understands and loves it himself. That lonely height of love and understanding is necessary, by Nature's clumsy law, to produce a lower type; the great and noble are used as the means to the small and ignoble. Nature is a bad manager; her expenses are far greater than her profits: for all her riches she must one day go bankrupt. She would have acted more reasonably to make the rule of her household— small expense and hundredfold profit; if there had been, for example, only a few artists with moderate powers, but an immense number of hearers to appreciate them, stronger and more powerful characters than the artists themselves; then the effect of the art-work, in comparison with the cause, might be a hundred-tongued echo. One might at least expect cause and effect to be of equal power; but Nature lags infinitely behind this consummation. An artist, and especially a philosopher, seems often to have dropped by chance into his age, as a wandering hermit or straggler cut off from the main body. Think how utterly great Schopenhauer is, and what a small and absurd effect he has had! An honest man can feel no greater shame at the present time than at the thought of the casual treatment Schopenhauer has received and the evil powers

that have up to now killed his effect among men.
First there was the want of readers,—to the eternal
shame of our cultivated age ;—then the inadequacy
of his first public adherents, as soon as he had any ;
further, I think, the crassness of the modern man
towards books, which he will no longer take
seriously.   As an outcome of many attempts to
adapt Schopenhauer to this enervated age, the new
danger has gradually arisen of regarding him as an
odd kind of pungent herb, of taking him in grains,
as a sort of metaphysical pepper.   In this way he
has gradually become famous, and I should think
more have heard his name than Hegel's ; and, for
all that, he is still a solitary being, who has failed
of his effect.—Though the honour of causing the
failure belongs least of all to the barking of his
literary antagonists ; first because there are few
men with the patience to read them, and secondly,
because any one who does, is sent immediately to
Schopenhauer himself; for who will let a donkey-
driver prevent him from mounting a fine horse,
however much he praise his donkey ?

Whoever has recognised Nature's unreason in our
time, will have to consider some means to help her ;
his task will be to bring the free spirits and the
sufferers from this age to know Schopenhauer ;
and make them tributaries to the flood that is to
overbear all the clumsy uses to which Nature even
now is accustomed to put her philosophers.   Such
men will see that the identical obstacles hinder the
effect of a great philosophy and the production of
the great philosopher ; and so will direct their aims
to prepare the regeneration of Schopenhauer, which

means that of the philosophical genius. The real opposition to the further spread of his doctrine in the past, and the regeneration of the philosopher in the future, is the perversity of human nature as it is; and all the great men that are to be must spend infinite pains in freeing themselves from it. The world they enter is plastered over with pretence— including not merely religious dogmas, but such juggling conceptions as "progress," "universal education," "nationalism," "the modern state"; practically all our general terms have an artificial veneer over them that will bring a clearer-sighted posterity to reproach our age bitterly for its warped and stunted growth, however loudly we may boast of our "health." The beauty of the antique vases, says Schopenhauer, lies in the simplicity with which they express their meaning and object; it is so with all the ancient implements; if Nature produced amphoræ, lamps, tables, chairs, helmets, shields, breastplates and the like, they would resemble these. And, as a corollary, whoever considers how we all manage our art, politics, religion and educa- tion—to say nothing of our vases!—will find in them a barbaric exaggeration and arbitrariness of expression. Nothing is more unfavourable to the rise of genius than such monstrosities. They are unseen and undiscoverable, the leaden weights on his hand when he will set it to the plough; the weights are only shaken off with violence, and his highest work must to an extent always bear the mark of it.

In considering the conditions that, at best, keep the born philosopher from being oppressed by the perversity of the age, I am surprised to find they are partly those in which Schopenhauer himself grew up. True, there was no lack of opposing influences; the evil time drew perilously near him in the person of a vain and pretentious mother. But the proud republican character of his father rescued him from her and gave him the first quality of a philosopher—a rude and strong virility. His father was neither an official nor a savant; he travelled much abroad with his son,—a great help to one who must know men rather than books, and worship truth before the state. In time he got accustomed to national peculiarities: he made England, France and Italy equally his home, and felt no little sympathy with the Spanish character. On the whole, he did not think it an honour to be born in Germany, and I am not sure that the new political conditions would have made him change his mind. He held quite openly the opinion that the state's one object was to give protection at home and abroad, and even protection against its "protectors," and to attribute any other object to it was to endanger its true end. And so, to the consternation of all the so-called liberals, he left his property to the survivors of the Prussian soldiers who fell in 1848 in the fight for order. To understand the state and its duties in this single sense may seem more and more henceforth the sign of intellectual superiority; for the man with the *furor philosophicus* in him will no longer have time for the *furor politicus*, and will wisely keep from reading the newspapers or serving a party; though he will not hesitate a moment to take his place in the ranks if his country be in real need. All states are badly managed, when other men than politicians busy themselves with politics; and they deserve to be ruined by their political amateurs.

Schopenhauer had another great advantage— that he had never been educated for a professor, but worked for some time (though against his will) as a merchant's clerk, and through all his early years breathed the freer air of a great commercial house. A savant can never become a philosopher: Kant himself could not, but remained in a chrysalis stage to the end, in spite of the innate force of his genius. Any one who thinks I do Kant wrong in saying this does not know what a philosopher is— not only a great thinker, but also a real man; and how could a real man have sprung from a savant? He who lets conceptions, opinions, events, books come between himself and things, and is born for history (in the widest sense), will never see anything at once, and never be himself a thing to be "seen at once"; though both these powers should be in the philosopher, as he must take most of his doctrine from himself and be himself the copy and compendium of the whole world. If a man look at himself through a veil of other people's opinions, no wonder he sees nothing but—those opinions. And it is thus that the professors see and live. But Schopenhauer had the rare happiness of seeing the genius not only in himself, but also outside himself—in Goethe; and this double re-flection taught him everything about the aims and culture of the learned. He knew by this experience how the free strong man, to whom all artistic culture was looking, must come to be born; and could he, after this vision, have much desire to busy himself with the so-called " art," in the learned, hypocritical manner of the moderns?   He had seen something higher than that—an awful unearthly judgment-scene in which all life, even the highest and completest, was weighed and found too light; he had beheld the saint as the judge of existence.   We cannot tell how early Schopenhauer reached this view of life, and came to hold it with such intensity as to make all his writings an attempt to mirror it; we know that the youth had this great vision, and can well believe it of the child.   Everything that he gained later from life and books, from all the realms of knowledge, was only a means of colour and expression to him ;   the Kantian philosophy itself was to him an extraordinary rhetorical instrument for making the utterance of his vision, as he thought, clearer; the Buddhist and Christian mythologies occasionally served the same end.   He had one task and a thousand means to execute it ; one meaning, and innumerable hieroglyphs to express it.

It was one of the high conditions of his existence that he really could live for such a task—according to his motto *vitam impendere vero* — and none of life's material needs could shake his resolution ; and we know the splendid return he made his father for this.   The contemplative man in Germany usually pursues his scientific studies to the detriment of his sincerity, as a " considerate fool," in search of place and honour, circumspect and obsequious, and fawning on his influential superiors.

Nothing offended the savants more than Schopenhauer's unlikeness to them.

VIII.

These are a few of the conditions under which
the philosophical genius can at least come to light
in our time, in spite of all thwarting influences;—
a virility of character, an early knowledge of
mankind, an absence of learned education and
narrow patriotism, of compulsion to earn his
livelihood or depend on the state,—freedom in
fact, and again freedom; the same marvellous and
dangerous element in which the Greek philosophers
grew up. The man who will reproach him, as
Niebuhr did Plato, with being a bad citizen, may
do so, and be himself a good one; so he and
Plato will be right together! Another may call
this great freedom presumption; he is also right,
as he could not himself use the freedom properly
if he desired it, and would certainly presume too
far with it. This freedom is really a grave burden
of guilt; and can only be expiated by great
actions. Every ordinary son of earth has the
right of looking askance on such endowments;
and may Providence keep him from being so
endowed—burdened, that is, with such terrible
duties! His freedom and his loneliness would be
his ruin, and ennui would turn him into a fool, and
a mischievous fool at that.

A father may possibly learn something from
this that he may use for his son's private education,

though one must not expect fathers to have only philosophers for their sons. It is possible that they will always oppose their sons becoming philosophers, and call it mere perversity ; Socrates was sacrificed to the fathers' anger, for "corrupting the youth," and Plato even thought a new ideal state necessary to prevent the philosophers' growth from being dependent on the fathers' folly. It looks at present as though Plato had really accomplished something; for the modern state counts the encouragement of philosophy as one of its duties and tries to secure for a number of men at a time the sort of freedom that conditions the philosopher.   But, historically, Plato has been very unlucky; as soon as a structure has risen corresponding actually to his proposals, it has always turned, on a closer view, into a goblin-child, a monstrous changeling ; compare the ecclesiastical state of the Middle Ages with the government of the "God-born king" of which Plato dreamed ! The modern state is furthest removed from the idea of the Philosopher-king (Thank Heaven for that! the Christian will say); but we must think whether it takes that very "encouragement of philosophy" in a Platonic sense, I mean as seriously and honestly as if its highest object were to produce more Platos. If the philosopher seem, as usual, an accident of his time, does the state make it its conscious business to turn the accidental into the necessary and help Nature here also ?

Experience teaches us a better way—or a worse : it says that nothing so stands in the way of the birth and growth of Nature's philosopher as the bad philosophers made "by order." A poor obstacle, isn't it? and the same that Schopenhauer pointed out in his famous essay on University philosophy. I return to this point, as men must be forced to take it seriously, to be driven to activity by it; and I think all writing is useless that does not contain such a stimulus to activity. And anyhow it is a good thing to apply Schopenhauer's eternal theories once more to our own contemporaries, as some kindly soul might think that everything has changed for the better in Germany since his fierce diatribes. Unfortunately his work is incomplete on this side as well, unimportant as the side may be.

The "freedom" that the state, as I said, bestows on certain men for the sake of philosophy is, properly speaking, no freedom at all, but an office that maintains its holder. The "encouragement of philosophy" means that there are to-day a number of men whom the state enables to make their living out of philosophy; whereas the old sages of Greece were not paid by the state, but at best were presented, as Zeno was, with a golden crown and a monument in the Ceramicus. I cannot say generally whether truth is served by showing the way to live by her, since everything depends on the character of the individual who shows the way. I can imagine a degree of pride in a man saying to his fellow-men, "take care of me, as I have something better to do—namely to take care of you." We should not be angry at such a heightened mode of expression in Plato and Schopenhauer; and so they might properly

have been University philosophers,—as Plato, for
example, was a court philosopher for a while
without lowering the dignity of philosophy. But
in Kant we have the usual submissive professor,
without any nobility in his relations with the
state; and thus he could not justify the University
philosophy when it was once assailed. If there be
natures like Schopenhauer's and Plato's, which can
justify it, I fear they will never have the chance, as
the state would never venture to give such men
these positions, for the simple reason that every
state fears them, and will only favour philosophers
it does not fear. The state obviously has a special
fear of philosophy, and will try to attract more
philosophers, to create the impression that it has
philosophy on its side,—because it has those men
on its side who have the title without the power.
But if there should come one who really proposes
to cut everything to the quick, the state included,
with the knife of truth, the state, that affirms its
own existence above all, is justified in banishing
him as an enemy, just as it bans a religion that
exalts itself to be its judge. The man who con-
sents to be a state philosopher, must also consent
to be regarded as renouncing the search for truth
in all its secret retreats. At any rate, so long as
he enjoys his position, he must recognise something higher than truth—the state. And not only
the state, but everything required by it for existence
—a definite form of religion, a social system, a
standing army; a *noli me tangere* is written
above all these things. Can a University
philosopher ever keep clearly before him the

whole round of these duties and limitations? I do not know. The man who has done so and remains a state-official, is a false friend to truth; if he has not,—I think he is no friend to truth either.

But general considerations like these are always the weakest in their influence on mankind. Most people will find it enough to shrug their shoulders and say, " As if anything great and pure has ever been able to maintain itself on this earth without some concession to human vulgarity! Would you rather the state persecuted philosophers than paid them for official services?" Without answering this last question, I will merely say that these " concessions" of philosophy to the state go rather far at present. In the first place, the state chooses its own philosophical servants, as many as its institutions require; it therefore pretends to be able to distinguish the good and the bad philosophers, and even assumes there must be a sufficient supply of good ones to fill all the chairs. The state is the authority not only for their goodness but their numbers. Secondly, it confines those it has chosen to a definite place and a definite activity among particular men; they must instruct every undergraduate who wants instruction, daily, at stated hours. The question is whether a philosopher can bind himself, with a good conscience, to have something to teach every day, to any one who wishes to listen. Must he not appear to know more than he does, and speak, before an unknown audience, of things that he could mention without risk only to his most intimate friends? And above all, does he not surrender the precious freedom of following his genius when and wherever it call him, by the mere fact of being bound to think at stated times on a fixed subject? And before young men, too! Is not such thinking in its nature emasculate? And suppose he felt some day that he had no ideas just then—and yet must be in his place and appear to be thinking! What then?

"But," one will say, "he is not a thinker but mainly a depository of thought, a man of great learning in all previous philosophies. Of these he can always say something that his scholars do not know." This is actually the third, and the most dangerous, concession made by philosophy to the state, when it is compelled to appear in the form of erudition, as the knowledge (more specifically) of the history of philosophy. The genius looks purely and lovingly on existence, like a poet, and cannot dive too deep into it;—and nothing is more abhorrent to him than to burrow among the innumerable strange and wrong-headed opinions. The learned history of the past was never a true philosopher's business, in India or Greece; and a professor of philosophy who busies himself with such matters must be, at best, content to hear it said of him, " He is an able scholar, antiquary, philologist, historian,"—but never, " He is a philosopher." I said, " at best": for a scholar feels that most of the learned works written by University philosophers are badly done, without any real scientific power, and generally are dreadfully tedious. Who will blow aside, for example, the Lethean vapour with which the history of

Greek philosophy has been enveloped by the dull though not very scientific works of Ritter, Brandis and Zeller? I, at any rate, would rather read Diogenes Laertius than Zeller, because at least the spirit of the old philosophers lives in Diogenes, but neither that nor any other spirit in Zeller. And, after all, what does the history of philosophy matter to our young men? Are they to be discouraged by the welter of opinions from having any of their own; or taught to join the chorus that approves the vastness of our progress? Are they to learn to hate or perhaps despise philosophy? One might expect the last, knowing the torture the students endure for their philosophical examinations, in having to get into their unfortunate heads the maddest efforts of the human mind as well as the greatest and profoundest. The only method of criticising a philosophy that is possible and proves anything at all—namely to see whether one can live by it—has never been taught at the universities; only the criticism of words, and again words, is taught there. Imagine a young head, without much experience of life, being stuffed with fifty systems (in the form of words) and fifty criticisms of them, all mixed up together,—what an overgrown wilderness he will come to be, what contempt he will feel for a philosophical education! It is, of course, not an education in philosophy at all, but in the art of passing a philosophical examination: the usual result being the pious ejaculation of the wearied examinee, "Thank God I am no philosopher, but a Christian and a good citizen!"

What if this cry were the ultimate object of the state, and the "education" or leading *to* philosophy were merely a leading *from* philosophy? We may well ask.—But if so, there is one thing to fear— that the youth may some day find out to what end philosophy is thus mis-handled. "Is the highest thing of all, the production of the philosophical genius, nothing but a pretext, and the main object perhaps to hinder his production? And is Reason turned to Unreason?"—Then woe to the whole machinery of political and professorial trickery!

Will it soon become notorious? I do not know; but anyhow university philosophy has fallen into a general state of doubting and despair. The cause lies partly in the feebleness of those who hold the chairs at present: and if Schopenhauer had to write his treatise on university philosophy to-day, he would find the club no longer necessary, but could conquer with a bulrush. They are the heirs and successors of those slip-shod thinkers whose crazy heads Schopenhauer struck at: their childish natures and dwarfish frames remind one of the Indian proverb: "men are born according to their deeds, deaf, dumb, misshapen." Those fathers deserved such sons, "according to their deeds," as the proverb says. Hence the students will, no doubt, soon get on without the philosophy taught at their university, just as those who are not university men manage to do without it already. This can be tested from one's own experience: in my student-days, for example, I found the university philosophers very ordinary men indeed,

who had collected together a few conclusions from
the other sciences, and in their leisure hours read
the newspapers and went to concerts; they were
treated by their academic colleagues with politely
veiled contempt.   They had the reputation of
knowing very little, but of never being at a loss for
obscure expressions to conceal their ignorance.
They had a preference for those obscure regions
where a man could not walk long with clear
vision.   One said of the natural sciences,—"Not
one of them can fully explain to me the origin of
matter; then what do I care about them all?"—
Another said of history, "It tells nothing new to
the man with ideas": in fact, they always found
reasons for its being more philosophical to know
nothing than to learn anything.   If they let themselves be drawn to learn, a secret instinct made
them fly from the actual sciences and found a dim
kingdom amid their gaps and uncertainties.   They
"led the way" in the sciences in the sense that the
quarry "leads the way" for the hunters who are
behind him.   Recently they have amused themselves with asserting they are merely the watchers
on the frontier of the sciences.   The Kantian
doctrine is of use to them here, and they industriously build up an empty scepticism on it, of which
in a short time nobody will take any more notice.
Here and there one will rise to a little metaphysic
of his own, with the general accompaniment of
headaches and giddiness and bleeding at the nose
After the usual ill-success of their voyages into the
clouds and the mist, some hard-headed young
student of the real sciences will pluck them down

by the skirts, and their faces will assume the expression now habitual to them, of offended dignity at being found out. They have lost their happy confidence, and not one of them will venture a step further for the sake of his philosophy. Some used to believe they could find out new religions or reinstate old ones by their systems. They have given up such pretensions now, and have become mostly mild, muddled folk, with no Lucretian boldness, but merely some spiteful complaints of the "dead weight that lies on the intellects of mankind"! No one can even learn logic from them now, and their obvious knowledge of their own powers has made them discontinue the dialectical disputations common in the old days. There is much more care and modesty, logic and inventiveness, in a word, more philosophical method in the work of the special sciences than in the so-called "philosophy," and every one will agree with the temperate words of Bagehot * on the present system builders : "Unproved abstract principles without number have been eagerly caught up by sanguine men, and then carefully spun out into books and theories, which were to explain the whole world. But the world goes clear against these abstractions, and it must do so, as they require it to go in antagonistic directions. The mass of a system attracts the young and impresses the unwary ; but cultivated people are very

---

* *Physics and Politics*, chap. v. Nietzsche has altered the order of the sentences without any apparent benefit to his own argument, and to the disadvantage of Bagehot's. I have restored the original order.—TR.

dubious about it. They are ready to receive hints and suggestions, and the smallest real truth is ever welcome. But a large book of deductive philosophy is much to be suspected. Who is not almost sure beforehand that the premises will contain a strange mixture of truth and error, and therefore that it will not be worth while to spend life in reasoning over their consequences?" The philosophers, especially in Germany, used to sink into such a state of abstraction that they were in continual danger of running their heads against a beam; but there is a whole herd of Laputan flappers about them to give them in time a gentle stroke on their eyes or anywhere else. Sometimes the blows are too hard; and then these scorners of earth forget themselves and strike back, but the victim always escapes them. "Fool, you do not see the beam," says the flapper; and often the philosopher does see the beam, and calms down. These flappers are the natural sciences and history; little by little they have so overawed the German dream-craft which has long taken the place of philosophy, that the dreamer would be only too glad to give up the attempt to run alone: but when they unexpectedly fall into the others' arms, or try to put leading-strings on them that they may be led themselves, those others flap as terribly as they can, as if they would say, " This is all that is wanting,—that a philosophaster like this should lay his impure hands on us, the natural sciences and history! Away with him!" Then they start back, knowing not where to turn or to ask the way. They wanted to have a little physical knowledge at their back, possibly in the form of empirical psychology (like the Herbartians), or perhaps a little history; and then they could at least make a public show of behaving scientifically, although in their hearts they may wish all philosophy and all science at the devil.

But granted that this herd of bad philosophers is ridiculous—and who will deny it?—how far are they also harmful?   They are harmful just because they make philosophy ridiculous.   As long as this imitation-thinking continues to be recognised by the state, the lasting effect of a true philosophy will be destroyed, or at any rate circumscribed; nothing does this so well as the curse of ridicule that the representatives of the great cause have drawn on them, for it attacks that cause itself. And so I think it will encourage culture to deprive philosophy of its political and academic standing, and relieve state and university of the task, impossible for them, of deciding between true and false philosophy.   Let the philosophers run wild, forbid them any thoughts of office or civic position, hold them out no more bribes,—nay, rather persecute them and treat them ill,—you will see a wonderful result.   They will flee in terror and seek a roof where they can, these poor phantasms; one will become a parson, another a schoolmaster, another will creep into an editorship, another write school-books for young ladies' colleges, the wisest of them will plough the fields, the vainest go to court. Everything will be left suddenly empty, the birds flown : for it is easy to get rid of bad philosophers, —one only has to cease paying them.   And that

N*

is a better plan than the open patronage of any philosophy, whatever it be, for state reasons.

The state has never any concern with truth, but only with the truth useful to it, or rather, with anything that is useful to it, be it truth, half-truth, or error. A coalition between state and philosophy has only meaning when the latter can promise to be unconditionally useful to the state, to put its well-being higher than truth. It would certainly be a noble thing for the state to have truth as a paid servant; but it knows well enough that it is the essence of truth to be paid nothing and serve nothing. So the state's servant turns out to be merely "false truth," a masked actor who cannot perform the office required from the real truth— the affirmation of the state's worth and sanctity. When a mediæval prince wished to be crowned by the Pope, but could not get him to consent, he appointed an antipope to do the business for him. This may serve up to a certain point; but not when the modern state appoints an "anti-philosophy" to legitimise it; for it has true philosophy against it just as much as before, or even more so. I believe in all seriousness that it is to the state's advantage to have nothing further to do with philosophy, to demand nothing from it, and let it go its own way as much as possible. Without this indifferent attitude, philosophy may become dangerous and oppressive, and will have to be persecuted.—The only interest the state can have in the university lies in the training of obedient and useful citizens; and it should hesitate to put this obedience and usefulness in doubt by demanding an examination in philosophy from the young men.   To make a bogey of philosophy may be an excellent way to frighten the idle and incompetent from its study; but this advantage is not enough to counterbalance the danger that this kind of compulsion may arouse from the side of the more reckless and turbulent spirits.   They learn to know about forbidden books, begin to criticise their teachers, and finally come to understand the object of university philosophy and its examinations; not to speak of the doubts that may be fostered in the minds of young theologians, as a consequence of which they are beginning to be extinct in Germany, like the ibexes in the Tyrol.

I know the objections that the state could bring against all this, as long as the lovely Hegel-corn was yellowing in all the fields; but now that hail has destroyed the crop and all men's hopes of it, now that nothing has been fulfilled and all the barns are empty,—there are no more objections to be made, but rather rejections of philosophy itself.   The state has now the power of rejection; in Hegel's time it only wished to have it—and that makes a great difference.   The state needs no more the sanction of philosophy, and philosophy has thus become superfluous to it.   It will find advantage in ceasing to maintain its professors, or (as I think will soon happen) in merely pretending to maintain them; but it is of still greater importance that the university should see the benefit of this as well.   At least I believe the real sciences must see that their interest lies

in freeing themselves from all contact with sham
science. And further, the reputation of the
universities hangs too much in the balance for
them not to welcome a severance from methods
that are thought little of even in academic circles.
The outer world has good reason for its widespread contempt of universities; they are re-
proached with being cowardly, the small fearing
the great, and the great fearing public opinion; it
is said that they do not lead the higher thought
of the age but hobble slowly behind it, and cleave
no longer to the fundamental ideas of the
recognised sciences. Grammar, for example, is
studied more diligently than ever without any one
seeing the necessity of a rigorous training in speech
and writing. The gates of Indian antiquity are
being opened, and the scholars have no more idea
of the most imperishable works of the Indians—
their philosophies—than a beast has of playing
the harp; though Schopenhauer thinks that the
acquaintance with Indian philosophy is one of the
greatest advantages possessed by our century.
Classical antiquity is the favourite playground
nowadays, and its effect is no longer classical and
formative; as is shown by the students, who are
certainly no models for imitation. Where is now
the spirit of Friedrich August Wolf to be found,
of whom Franz Passow could say that he seemed
a loyal and humanistic spirit with force enough
to set half the world aflame? Instead of that a
journalistic spirit is arising in the university, often
under the name of philosophy; the smooth
delivery—the very cosmetics of speech — with

Faust and Nathan the Wise for ever on the lips, the accent and the outlook of our worst literary magazines and, more recently, much chatter about our holy German music, and the demand for lectures on Schiller and Goethe,—all this is a sign that the university spirit is beginning to be confused with the Spirit of the Age. Thus the establishment of a higher tribunal, outside the universities, to protect and criticise them with regard to culture, would seem a most valuable thing, and as soon as philosophy can sever itself from the universities and be purified from every unworthy motive or hypocrisy, it will be able to become such a tribunal. It will do its work without state help in money or honours, free from the spirit of the age as well as from any fear of it; being in fact the judge, as Schopenhauer was, of the so-called culture surrounding it. And in this way the philosopher can also be useful to the university, by refusing to be a part of it, but criticising it from afar. Distance will lend dignity.

But, after all, what does the life of a state or the progress of universities matter in comparison with the life of philosophy on earth! For, to say quite frankly what I mean, it is infinitely more important that a philosopher should arise on the earth than that a state or a university should continue. The dignity of philosophy may rise in proportion as the submission to public opinion and the danger to liberty increase; it was at its highest during the convulsions marking the fall of the Roman Republic, and in the time of the Empire, when the names of both philosophy and history became *ingrata principibus nomina.* Brutus shows its dignity better than Plato; his was a time when ethics cease to have commonplaces. Philosophy is not much regarded now, and we may well ask why no great soldier or statesman has taken it up; and the answer is that a thin phantom has met him under the name of philosophy, the cautious wisdom of the learned professor; and philosophy has soon come to seem ridiculous to him. It ought to have seemed terrible; and men who are called to authority should know the heroic power that has its source there. An American may tell them what a centre of mighty forces a great thinker can prove on this earth. "Beware when the great God lets loose a thinker on this planet," says Emerson.* "Then all things are at risk. It is as when a conflagration has broken out in a great city, and no man knows what is safe, or where it will end. There is not a piece of science, but its flank may be turned to-morrow; there is not any literary reputation, not the so-called eternal names of fame, that may not be revised and condemned. . . . The things which are dear to men at this hour are so on account of the ideas which have emerged on their mental horizon, and which cause the present order of things as a tree bears its apples. A new degree of culture would instantly revolutionise the entire system of human pursuits." If such thinkers are dangerous, it is clear why our university thinkers are not dangerous; for their thoughts bloom as peacefully in the shade of tradition " as

* Essay on "Circles."

ever tree bore its apples." They do not frighten; they carry away no gates of Gaza; and to all their little contemplations one can make the answer of Diogenes when a certain philosopher was praised: "What great result has he to show, who has so long practised philosophy and yet has *hurt* nobody?" Yes, the university philosophy should have on its monument, "It has hurt nobody." But this is rather the praise one gives to an old woman than to a goddess of truth; and it is not surprising that those who know the goddess only as an old woman are the less men for that, and are naturally neglected by the real men of power.

If this be the case in our time, the dignity of philosophy is trodden in the mire; and she seems herself to have become ridiculous or insignificant. All her true friends are bound to bear witness against this transformation, at least to show that it is merely her false servants in philosopher's clothing who are so. Or better, they must prove by their own deed that the love of truth has itself awe and power.

Schopenhauer proved this and will continue to prove it, more and more.

Printed in the United States
134028LV00007B/112-129/A